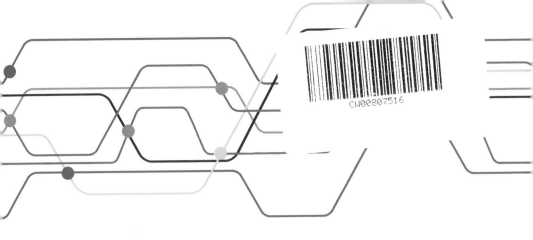

Excellent
IT Management

DAVID E McKEAN

About the Author and IT Leaders

DAVID MCKEAN IS A FORMER CIO WHO HAS WORKED FOR SEVERAL MULTINATIONAL COMPANIES AROUND THE WORLD. Through his work with over 1,000 course delegates and interviews with some of the top IT managers and CIOs worldwide, he knows what it takes to succeed as an IT professional.

Excellent IT Management looks at five key aspects of IT management: business planning and IT strategy, advanced project management and change leadership, operational performance, crisis management, and commercial IT management. The second book in the series, *Excellent IT Leadership*, looks at personal leadership, leading IT teams, building influence and valuable networks, technology innovation, and corporate IT leadership.

The books are the basis for the courses *Excellent IT Management* and *Excellent IT Leadership*, run globally through a network of partners, both as public and in-house courses and interactive, live online programs. They are based on the experiences of our delegates and additional interviewees.

If you have any comments or management learning that you would like to be considered for future editions, please feel free to e-mail David at david.mckean@itleaders.co.uk.

David McKean
IT Leaders, Greenlands, Henley-on-Thames,
Oxfordshire, RG9 3AU, UK
E-mail: david.mckean@itleaders.co.uk;
Telephone: +44 1491 57 86 88 (UK) or (+1) 203 810 6143 (US)

Contents

The Secret to Good IT Management

EXCELLENT IT MANAGEMENT **REVEALS THE SECRETS FOR OUT-STANDING IT MANAGEMENT TOGETHER WITH SOME TOOLS, TECH**-niques, and a coherent skills framework that has been five years in the making. This book is based on the experiences of more than one thousand senior IT managers and presents their guidelines for success. It also includes some of my own experiences, as well as expertise gained from my company IT Leaders and the numerous IT professionals with whom I have worked. This book presumes you are an experienced IT manager and are looking for new ideas to enhance your career success.

The development of IT management skills presents a constant dilemma. Many IT managers come from jobs that relied on technical skills that now count for little in their new management role. Some respond by "keeping their hand in"—in other words, interfering. They get frustrated because they perceive themselves to be less valuable than they were before. As one manager put it, "It feels like I was chosen for the tennis team because I was once good at swimming."

BEN'S STORY: WHAT NOW, BOSS?

I remember vividly my first job as an IT director. I was working for a large organization in Cape Town, South Africa. I had arrived at my hotel at 2:00 a.m. after a long flight. My management team, seeking to impress me with their enthusiasm, had arranged to meet me at 8:00 a.m. the following morning.

I looked at them through bloodshot eyes as they asked eagerly, "What would you like us to do, boss?" It was a seminal moment for me. The plain truth was that I had no idea. The people around the table knew a lot more about what needed to be done than I did. As I found out later, new managers often have this feeling of being out of their depth, of feeling like a bit of a fraud. Apparently it is quite common and has a name—imposter syndrome. Clearly no new manager can ever possibly know everything from the outset. Fortunately in my case, I stumbled through by asking a number of smart questions, and I used the experience of the team to guide me.

IT management is very different from IT. To be successful you need to be constantly reviewing what you are doing and aligning it to business priorities. This is different from most IT jobs, where the work is clearly defined. Our analysis shows that success is about fulfilling a number of important roles in ever-changing proportions. There are ten roles in total; five are addressed as part of *Excellent IT Management* and the second five as part of *Excellent IT Leadership*.

The roles are as follows:

Excellent IT Management

1. IT strategist: putting together effective IT plans and strategies

2. Business change leader: working with business sponsors to deliver successful projects and business change

3. Performance pioneer: creating and delivering a culture of continual service improvement

4. Crisis commander: being prepared for the worst and leading from the front

5. Commercial expert: IT financial management, sourcing strategy, negotiating good IT contracts, and working successfully with IT partners

Excellent IT Leadership

1. Personal coach: making the most of your time, developing your style or "brand," and taking control of your career

2. Team captain: creating a culture of success and leading technology teams

3. Executive connector: networking effectively and influencing other senior managers

4. Technology innovator: understanding and promoting new and practical technologies

5. Business champion: working at the top level to lead the business forward

It is notable that all the CIOs interviewed for this book are avid readers. The footnotes throughout the book reference some excellent books that have been a source of inspiration to me and others.

This book is first and foremost a practical guide based on real experience. I hope it will give you some new ideas and inspire you to further success.

1. IT Strategist

1.1 DEFINITIONS OF STRATEGY

THE WORD *STRATEGY* CAN BE VERY CONFUSING. DIFFERENT PEO-PLE USE IT TO MEAN SLIGHTLY DIFFERENT THINGS. IT IS SOMETIMES used to mean a major activity, as in "one of our strategies is to implement SharePoint." Sometimes it is used to express a future outcome, such as "our strategy is to increase our international market share." We even hear some managers use it to mean "very important," as in "I am working on a strategic project for the board." Each of these uses is slightly erroneous. Strategy is not an activity or an outcome but in fact a combination of both. The *Merriam Webster Dictionary* defines strategy as follows:

> *Strategy (n):* a careful plan or method for achieving a particular goal usually over a long period of time

It is really important to grasp both components. So, at the risk of being repetitive, strategy has a long-term aim and (very importantly) a plan to get there. It is not uncommon to come across slightly different definitions. While it is difficult to say these are not correct, they are generally unhelpful in creating effective business or IT strategy.

The following amended definition originally given in *Strategy Fast Track to Success*[1] may also be helpful:

> *Strategy*: defining the best future for your organization, mapping the route to achieve it and communicating it clearly to the organization

There are four important aspects of this definition:

1. Strategy is about achieving the best future, not just the most obvious, the first idea you thought of, or an extrapolation of the past.

2. It has to be achievable.

3. There must be a clear and logical route to achieve it (the plan we mentioned earlier).

4. Finally, it must be communicated to the organization for it to become reality (not part of the formal definition, but I think we can all agree that a strategy is of no value if no one knows about it).

Never forget the real point of strategy, which is to help us achieve higher goals, more profit, bigger market share, or whatever the measure of success happens to be. What strategy does, therefore, is allow everyone to understand what the overall goals are, and hence, more specifically, what their roles would be in achieving them. Since there are usually many routes to achieve any end goal, it is important that everyone knows which path has been chosen. This means that everyone is working on the same activities rather than going off in different directions.

The term *end goal* rather than *end vision* is used deliberately. The word *vision* is often used in the context of strategy. So, just to be clear, vision is normally a high-level, sometimes emotive, and usually broad

---

1   *Strategy Fast Track to Success*, David McKean, published by Pearson

(i.e., vague) end goal. It is a useful guide to where the future lies. To realize the true value of strategy, though, the end goal needs to be defined with some quantified objectives.

A short footnote before we continue. This book focuses on creating an IT strategy to support the high-level business goals. We talk about nonIT departments as "the business." Although IT is clearly part of the business, the term is so widely used as to not be worth changing, and it is used in this same context here.

1.2 WHAT GOES WRONG WITH STRATEGY?

It sounds easy, doesn't it? Of course, it isn't. Many companies (probably the majority) have a strategy but do not receive the benefits. And, in my experience, the benefits on offer are massive. A company that creates and communicates a quality strategy can improve its performance by more than 20 percent. In many cases it is higher, and in some cases, it is the difference between success and failure. So before we go further, here is a short list of some of the things that can go wrong, as witnessed by other IT managers.

1.2.1 IT strategy in isolation

Some organizations believe that only the board of directors develops top-level strategy. And that only the IT department develops the IT strategy. Nothing could be further from the truth. It is true that both business and IT strategy call for some strong choices and should not be diluted by consensus and compromise. Even so, both still benefit from a collaborative process involving input from the board of directors, all business departments, and key members of the IT team.

1.2.2 An extension of past activities

If an IT department has been doing the same things for a number of years, it is easy to think that the same formula will work in the

future. The department confuses strategy (identifying the best future and mapping the route to achieve it) with long-term planning (an extrapolation of the past). A good example of this is where a strategy is produced on the basis of a budget that has been handed down by finance. It may be a request to reduce costs by 10 percent, for example. Crafting a strategy to meet this objective is dangerous in many ways. First of all, cost reductions may be only one of the high-level (i.e. corporate) goals. Second, it may be possible to achieve much more than is requested, or conversely, it may potentially seriously damage the company, if, for example, critical systems are neglected, or security compromised.

1.2.3 No structure or method

This lowers the probability of success. Often the people who are responsible for strategy have used different methods in the past. This can cause a misalignment in how strategy gets developed, and that can be very time-consuming. There must be a clear purpose and a structured process to follow. In the case of IT strategy, it is particularly important to align the activities of the IT department to the business, and if each is following a different process, this can be very frustrating.

1.2.4 Too long or too short

All too often people are too busy with day-to-day operations to stop and think, let alone plan the future. As individuals we may be too reactive, responding to one crisis or another. At the other extreme, strategy can be made too difficult, requiring senior management to be tied up full-time for days. This damages the day-to-day operation, and often the outputs from such assessments are too detailed to withstand the test of time. The right balance needs to be struck. Strategic planning needs to be kept apart from operational issues and carefully planned so it does not overly disrupt day-to-day activities.

1.2.5 Focusing on everything

Some companies treat strategy like they would New Year's resolutions, promising to be successful in areas that they have not been in the past. It becomes an additional list of things to do. An important aspect of strategy is not just what you do, but what you don't do. Organizations talk about focusing on many different things. By definition focus can only be applied to a small number of priorities. One of the most valuable approaches an IT manager can take is to give their business stakeholders a choice of what could be done and ask for those options to be listed in order of value or priority. It then becomes possible to suggest that a particular activity could be either postponed (the alternative most likely to be chosen) or canceled (less likely, but different from the first, only in that it sounds so permanent!).

1.2.6 Incorrect resources

One of the most common problems is where the strategy does not "add up." If you look at the process in figure 1 of section 1.3, you will see that there are three key alignment points. First of all the IT objectives need to align to the high-level business objectives. Second, the strategic projects need to be carefully chosen to align to the IT objectives, and finally the project resources required need to be aligned to the resources available.

For a strategy to be successful, it needs to be integrated. Business sponsors need to know how many of their resources are required for each initiative so that it is evident what can be done with existing resources and which need additional ones. All too often business stakeholders assume that the resource limitations only exist in IT. It is the role of the IT manager to explain the whole picture. By way of example, imagine a fictitious CRM system. In theory, with modern software development tools, the software screens and workflow could be substantially changed in an afternoon. If you have a large customer care department, though,

training the users may take months. In this case the balance of work is clearly with the business. This needs to be fully considered when IT strategies are developed.

1.2.7 Too high level

Strategy has to paint a high-level picture, but if it is not grounded in practice, it risks being unachievable or inappropriate. It also needs to create a sense of urgency and act as the catalyst to kick off the key projects. Practical considerations mean that these initiatives are done in order of priority. A clear plan will also tell the organization what is expected of individuals so that they can support it. This is an important step because it demonstrates that strategy is not a paper exercise, which in turn helps to gain commitment.

1.2.8 Not communicated

The best strategy in the world will count for nothing if it is not well communicated. Different types of communication are required for different audiences. Board presentations might require a detailed presentation of financial growth and investment. Presentations to a wider audience might focus more on telling stories that illustrate what success looks like in terms that people can relate to in their day-to-day work. A recent example from one of our clients springs to mind. A clear and concise strategy had been developed with a list of high-level objectives, corporate programs, priorities, and values. However, when the senior managers were polled, only half of them knew it existed, and only half of them could remember anything from it. To use an analogy, building a strategy without communicating it is a bit like building a racing bike and forgetting to put on the seat.

1.2.9 Inflexible

Strategy needs to be flexible and agile to quickly take advantage of new opportunities and threats. Reviewing strategy just once a year can often

be insufficient as market forces change quickly. Regular reviews of strategy are more effective than a large planning exercise once a year. One of the characteristics of successful IT managers is that they identify and stop activities that are either no longer relevant or not of a high priority.

1.2.10 No measures of success

Measuring the success of strategy is very important. Metrics must mean something to those who are responsible for delivering results. So, for example, many help desks have call answer time as one of the key metrics. If this is not combined with other quality metrics of first-time fix rates, for example, it can be counterproductive—answering calls quickly without solving user problems rather misses the point.

1.3 A PROCESS AND GUIDELINES FOR IT STRATEGY

There are many models for developing business strategy but few for IT strategy. The model shown here is one we have developed over many years. It provides a good structure for building a high-quality and business-aligned strategy. It consists of six phases:

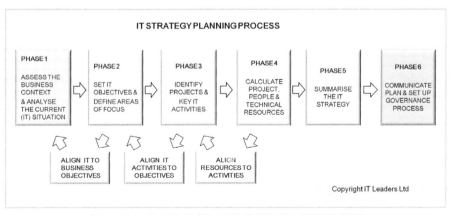

FIGURE 1. OUTLINE OF OUR IT STRATEGY PROCESS

Here are a few guidelines from the experiences of other IT managers that you may find helpful:

1.3.1 Choose your stakeholders carefully

With regard to stakeholders, choose carefully whom you include in your planning. Generally this will be the senior managers or directors. Check that there is representation from all of the key stakeholder groups with managers who will help align the strategy to the business priorities. Take care that you choose people who will contribute and support your planning activities.

Conversely, don't make the group too large. Restrict the number of stakeholders to make it easier to get agreement. Meet with your stakeholders early on in the process. Clarify their priorities, and agree on what they would like to see included in the plan. Outline the process you will be following and the time scale to complete each step.

1.3.2 Less is more

There is a lot of confusion around strategy. Managers create a lot of extra work for themselves to mask their confusion about what they are trying to achieve. Their hope is that among the various detailed documents, spreadsheets, and presentations, their bosses will be able to find what they need. And that is unfortunate because strategy is exactly the opposite of detail. You can be pretty sure that if you develop your plan at a detailed and granular level, you will have a list of tactics, not a high-level strategy. It is interesting to see how large IT consultancies in the past have provided clients with a set of templates to create strategy. Strategy cannot be done using templates. This approach fundamentally fails to grasp the heart of strategy, namely that it is high-level. Strategy is a top-down process, not bottom-up. Once the high-level plan is done, feel free to let the detail people get on with their spreadsheets and mega-slide presentations.

1.3.3 Keep it high-level

Strategy is about simple high-level clarity. If you do it right, a strategic plan can be created within a few days. In practice this is unlikely. However, when we work with businesses to develop their business or IT strategies, we set up four one-day workshops spaced two to three weeks apart. Although the thinking time is only a few days, the elapsed time is normally closer to two months. Stay at the high level while you are building the framework before adding the detail. If you include the detail at the beginning, you will have to redo it every time you make a change. As stated before, much better to do the high-level stuff first and then add the detail afterward.

1.3.4 Don't boil the ocean

When top strategy consultants start a new assignment, they will typically have a very good idea of what needs to be done within a day or two of starting an assignment. This can come as a surprise, given that they don't know much about the specifics of the business. They call this first idea an Initial Hypothesis,[2] and although they may spend several weeks verifying the data (or how else would they be able to make a living?), it is rare that they need to change it. Their approach is to bring in the experience they have gleaned from other clients and match it against your situation. Extending what works and what doesn't from similar situations elsewhere means they can quickly get somewhere close to the right solution (the initial hypothesis).

You, on the other hand, know your business better than anyone, so at a high level, sketch out what your plan might look like. Avoid theoretical navel-gazing. Move quickly to what you think the answer is, and then validate your findings. That is, get your management team and senior sponsors to validate your straw man. Don't go into a meeting and try to create the plan from scratch. You will probably end up at the same place, but boy will it take a long time!

1.3.5 Separate objectives from the means

In our strategy work, we make a very strong distinction between the outcome you are trying to achieve and the means to achieve it. So, for

---

2   *The McKinsey Way*, Ethan Rasiel, published by McGraw-Hill

example, the statement "we will reduce costs by consolidating three data centers to two" is not a pure objective as it has already stated how it will be achieved. Later in this chapter we describe this as a "strategic statement," i.e., a statement that combines the objective (reduce costs) with the means (consolidate data centers). So, to summarize, do not jump straight away to the solution. Identify your objectives first, look at all the options for achieving them, and then choose the most appropriate ones.

1.3.6 Keep looking for better ways

Look carefully at what is being proposed. The solutions put forward are certainly not the only ones that are possible and often not the best ones. So be on the lookout for solutions and ideas that aren't up to it, remembering that not all ideas are good ideas.

1.3.7 Things don't happen by magic

One of my biggest bugbears with many strategies is that they put forward bold targets but with no guidance as to how it they are to be achieved. To use the analogy of the strategy of war, it is not sufficient to say we are going to outflank our enemy and take them all prisoner. You need to know which battalions will take on the task and how they will get behind the enemy, and you need to be assured that you have the troops and weapons. So making bold statements about process efficiency gains and cost savings are worthless without a clear view as to how they will be achieved. Things won't happen by magic.

1.3.8 Strategy is not a perfect science

And finally, recognize that strategy is not a perfect science. It has a finite life as market conditions and business priorities change. The French have an expression that translates roughly to "perfection is the enemy of the good." Strategy was known as the "art of the general," and it is important to keep it that way.

1.4 WHAT YOU NEED TO KNOW ABOUT BUSINESS STRATEGY

This chapter summarizes six of my favorite references and thoughts from the world of business strategy. It is a selection of strategic thinking that you are likely to come across in company-wide discussions on strategy.

These points are as follows:

1. Three key strategic principles from Michael Porter's groundbreaking paper "What Is Strategy?"[3]

2. The Balanced Scorecard method for developing strategy: the process that Kaplan and Norton developed that uses their balanced score-card as the basis for a company-wide integrated strategy

3. The six Ps: a checklist for marketers to analyze products in different markets

4. Porter's five forces: a concept again developed by Michael Porter for assessing competitive advantage

5. Mission, vision, and values: three key entities for summarizing corporate strategy

6. The extended Ansoff matrix: a way to summarize strategy by showing strategic emphasis for different products in different markets

To put it in context, let's go back to our original definition. This was about defining the best future for the organization and mapping the route to achieve it. The diagram below shows our starting point A and the future situation B, which has been chosen as the best strategic choice from several options. In creating strategy, therefore, we need

---

3   "What Is Strategy?" Michael E Porter, *Harvard Business Review* (product no. 4134)

to measure point A (our current situation), define our target (point B), and work out the difference, which tells us what we need to do (the strategic plan).

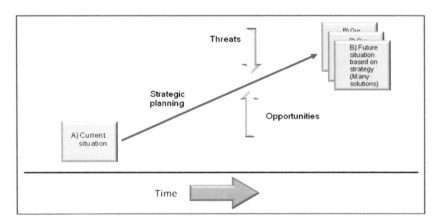

FIGURE 2. STRATEGY AT ITS SIMPLEST

1.4.1 Three principles for setting strategy

In his paper "What Is Strategy," Michael Porter identified three key principles for setting strategy:

1. Strategy is the creation of a unique and valuable position. Whenever you position your products, you will need them to have a competitive advantage over others, and the greater this competitive advantage, the more valuable will be your strategic position. Maintaining this competitive advantage is at the heart of all business strategy.

2. Strategy is about focus. You cannot expect to sell every product in every market, so you will need to make trade-offs in competing. This is all about focus, and of course by definition you cannot focus on many different things. Think of it as a bit like training for the Olympic Games; if you are undecided as to whether to enter the marathon or to enter the weightlifting competition and decide to train for both, you can guarantee that you will fail in both.

3. The final principle of setting strategy is to make sure that the future you define for your organization has a good fit in your company's activities. Although you may want to develop existing capabilities or move to new markets, it would be unrealistic to completely redesign everything you currently do and expect to be successful.

1.4.2 The Balanced Scorecard approach for developing strategy

In the 1970s and 1980s, companies were starting to recognize that focusing purely on the hard aspects of business was not necessarily the route to success. The work was started by Tanner Pascal and Athos, who wrote the book *The Art of Japanese Management*.[4] They identified that Japanese and Western companies were similar but differed in some important aspects. As a result they created the Seven S model. Essentially they recognized that some of the softer aspects of management, e.g. developing, motivating and leading people, were extremely important to long-term business success.

This theme was developed by Kaplan and Norton in the 1990s.[5] They recognized that an organization not only needed to take care of these softer issues, but they also needed to be measuring their performance in four specific areas:

1. Meeting customer needs and customer satisfaction
2. Internal business processes, which also includes information systems
3. Staff performance and their skills, learning, and growth
4. Financial performance

After Kaplan and Norton wrote their first successful book, *The Balanced Scorecard*, they also came to realize that many of their clients who had brought them in to develop a balanced scorecard were in fact really asking for help in developing their strategy. Their second book,

---

4   *The Art of Japanese Management*, Richard Tanner Pascale and Anthony Athos
5   *The Balanced Scorecard*, Robert Kaplan and David Norton

The Strategy-Focused Organization,[6] put together a very tidy model for developing strategy. It essentially described a four-step process:

1. Identify the key (balanced scorecard) objectives at the corporate level
2. Define a number of corporate programs (large projects) to achieve these
3. Create departmental objectives that have a "line of sight" to these programs and hence the corporate objectives
4. Cascade these to the individual employees' objectives

I have been fortunate to have worked for a company that adopted this high-level approach. The end results that the business delivered were extraordinary and were helped enormously by the clear and concise process.

1.4.3 The Six Ps

Let us move on to the next step, analyzing our current situation. One model often used by marketing is the six Ps model. This evaluates how well each of our products is operating in each market segment and is an important analysis tool for any high-level strategic discussion.

The six Ps analysis is a marketing tool that starts by looking at the following:

1. Place: in other words the marketplace where each product is targeted
2. Promotion: what is the best way to promote and sell the product (advertising, direct sales, etc.)
3. Product features: what features are most valuable for which market
4. Processes required for effective sales (for example, sales, customer care, etc.)
5. People and their knowledge and skills
6. Pricing: elasticity, discounting structures, etc.

---

6   *The Strategy-Focused Organization*, Robert Kaplan and David Norton

1.4.4 Competitive advantage

Another useful assessment of the current situation uses a model, again developed by Michael Porter, called Porter's five forces. The model looks at the market forces on each product, which in turn give an indication of its competitive advantage.

1. The first force is direct competition. Clearly the less competition the better. However, if there is no competition, you might want to ask why. Rather perversely, having competitors around can be quite reassuring!

2. The second question relates to new entrants. Even if there are no competitors today, how easy would it be for new competitors to set up and take a share of your market? Obviously, the more difficult the better. This is called the barrier to entry. High barriers to entry usually come about because a large up-front investment or specialist skills are needed.

3. The third question relates to what are called substitutes. A substitute is not a direct competitor but rather another product that competes for the same customer spend. A good example might be cinemas and restaurants. Clearly they are not direct competitors in that if you want to go out for dinner you will go to a restaurant and if you want to watch a movie you will go to the cinema. But they are substitute competitors because they are competing for the same entertainment spend.

4. The fourth force is that wielded by suppliers. Do you have products that are dependent on a small number of suppliers? If so this will count as a strong force. Ideally you want lots of suppliers so that you can get competitive pricing and keep your costs low.

5. Finally the fifth force is that created by customers. You want many customers to buy your products.

So to summarize you will have a high competitive advantage if you have low levels of competition from direct competitors, new entrants, or substitute competitors, as well as a large number of possible suppliers and a large potential customer base.

1.4.5 Mission, vision, and values

In the last two sections, we have looked at assessing the current situation. Now we move on to defining the future. Define the future situation at both a high level as well as at a more granular level (via quantified objectives). Mission, vision, and values are a very common guide for expressing the future at the high level. There is a fourth, namely competitive advantage.

1. The mission defines what your organization is going to do, as in Mission Impossible, e.g., "your mission, should you choose to accept it, is to…" The only difference is that in business, you aren't usually offered the choice!

2. Vision is the high-level view of what your organization (or indeed the market) will look like in the future. In researching the book *Strategy Fast Track to Success*, it was evident that many companies do not make a clear distinction between mission and vision. In the grand schema, these are of limited importance. It is much more important is have clear strategic end goals and for employees to understand what needs to be done.

3. Values are about the model behaviors and guiding beliefs of the organization with clear evidence that they are adhered to. For example, it would not be credible to have a set of beliefs that talk about valuing employees if the company has a reputation for laying people off.

4. Competitive advantage: Going back to the principles of focus and the idea that you have to choose your specialization, you need to be clear on what your organization does that really sets it apart. This area of expertise or excellence will be right at the heart of your

competitive advantage. A similar concept was identified as "driving force" by Tregoe and Zimmerman in their book *Top Level Strategy*.[7] This is a really excellent (and short) book on the essence of strategy.

Finally, make a note of the key assumptions that your business strategy is founded on. They may include predictions about market changes or the effectiveness of technology, or they could be statements that certain things will endure. Either way, when you review your strategy in the future and there is evidence that these assumptions no longer hold true, then review the strategy.

1.4.6 The extended Ansoff matrix and strategic emphasis

Returning to the wisdom of Michael Porter, one of his key insights was recognizing that all of a company's activities are ultimately directed to its products and markets. He recognized that you could effectively identify the strategy of any company by looking at how it will change the products it sells and the markets it will sell to. From this he concluded that the most fundamental strategic question is "What should the scope of our products and markets be?"

One of the best ways to represent this is with an extended Ansoff matrix. An example of this is shown in figure 3. The diagram has a number of different rows, each of which represents a group of products or services. How you group your products and services together is entirely your own decision. It requires enough groups to make the analysis useful but not so many that it becomes unwieldy.

We then have a number of different columns, each of which represents a particular market segment or group of customers. In some extreme situations, one can in fact represent one particularly large or valuable customer with its own column. Again how you divide and segment your markets is entirely up to you. Look for the market segments to be autonomous, in

---

7   *Top Level Strategy*, Tregoe and Zimmerman

other words not overlapping each other. Markets can segment in different ways; examples include segmenting by region, age, or customer value.

Products and services divide into three types. You have current products, modified products, and new products. The market divides in a similar way, so you have the markets that you currently serve, extended markets that you could move into, and indeed new markets. The matrix now divides into what are called product market cells. In the example here, three current product groups and three current market segments give us nine product market cells. These are the ones in the top left of the diagram and represent our current business.

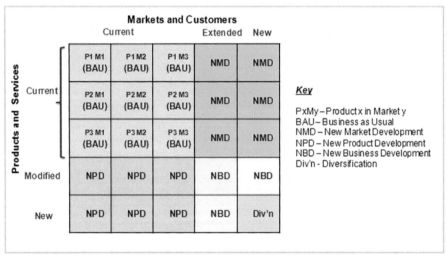

FIGURE 3. SEGMENTING PRODUCTS AND MARKETS

In fact, the diagram shows five product market groups in total. Your overall marketing strategy can be defined in terms of the emphasis across the Ansoff matrix. There are seven broad strategic options:

1. Maintain a steady course: this is where we continue to sell our existing products to our existing markets.

2. Rationalization: this is where you either stop selling certain products or reduce the number of markets you operate in.

3. Modify or create new products to sell into the current markets. In the diagram these are shown in blue, and these cells represent new product development.

4. Extend the markets of the existing product portfolio by launching into extended or new markets. These are shown in pink and represent new market developments.

5. Sell modified products into the extended and new markets, or sell modified and new products into extended markets. This is shown in green and represents new business development.

6. Diversification: selling new products into new markets

7. A combination of the above (the most usual choice)

You might find it interesting to evaluate your own organization in terms of this Ansoff matrix. When you have identified your product groups and market segmentation, look at each of the products' market cells in turn.

For each cell, think about whether it is expected to grow, stay flat, or reduce in size. Mark the cell with an arrow pointing upward if you think the cell will grow, a horizontal arrow for flat growth, and an arrow pointing downward if the market will reduce in importance. If you think you should exit from selling into that particular cell, mark it with a zero. If no revenue currently exists or will exist for that cell in the future, then mark it with an x. The diagram below gives an example of a company that is looking to do the following:

1. Grow all existing products in market 3
2. Grow product 1 into an extended and new market
3. Develop a new and extended product for existing market 1
4. Stay out of any other markets

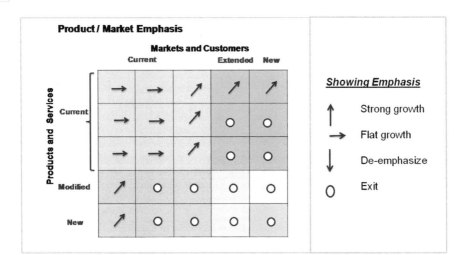

FIGURE 4. THE ANSOFF MATRIX SHOWING
EMPHASIS OF PRODUCTS AND MARKETS

1.5 IT STRATEGY STEP 1: GETTING YOUR BEARINGS

1.5.1 The business context

The previous section talked about some ideas for developing business strategy to give us confidence in getting involved in the process. To create a good IT strategy, it goes without saying that we need to know the business context. And it would be easy to assume that we can find this from the business strategy. In practice, though, this is often not the case. The IT department is frequently (in about half of cases, from our experience) required to develop the IT strategy without any clear top-level strategy. Even so, if we are smart, we should still be able to create one.

One of the most common questions that arises out of the creation of IT strategy is "What information does the IT department need to know in order to create a fully aligned business strategy?" The answer, of course, depends, but invariably it is less than most people think. Yes, it would be nice to understand the high-level strategic themes and the detailed corporate objectives and priorities. But practical experience tells us that this is rarely what we get. In our view you need the following information (in descending order of usefulness):

1. A full high-level corporate strategy
2. The high-level goals for the period ahead
3. The plans and goals of the individual heads of department
4. Corporate programs
5. Mission, vision, and values

Even if there is a clear strategy at the high level, you also need to have sight of the individual departmental strategies, e.g., the sales and marketing or customer care department's strategies. One of the most important things you can to do before rushing into creating an IT strategy is to meet with each of the key stakeholders in order to understand their plans and priorities for the period ahead. And, if they do not have a clear picture in mind, it is the job of the IT manager to put (IT-related) ideas forward for discussion and subsequent agreement. Ask them how well they think you are doing and what they are looking for from the IT department in the future. What aspects of what you provide for them today can be improved? Which of today's projects are invaluable, which are high priority, and which are of a lower priority? Are there indeed any projects that can be stopped or delayed?

In parallel with gaining a good understanding of the business context, it is necessary to take stock of how well you are performing as an organization. We suggest three techniques: the strategic canvass, PESTEL, and finally a SWOT analysis to bring everything together.

1.5.2 Strategic canvass

The concept of the strategic canvass was originally put forward by Kim and Mauborgne[8] in the *Harvard Business Review*. The ideas were developed further in their book *Blue Ocean Strategy*.[9]

---

8   "Charting Your Company's Future," Kim W.C. and R. Mauborgne, *Harvard Business Review*, 2002

9   *Blue Ocean Strategy*, Kim W.C. and R. Mauborgne, Harvard Business School Press

Their technique allows you to quickly see how you are performing against, say, six to ten key criteria. Once you have identified the most important criteria for your stakeholders or users, you need to measure how well you perform against them. These can then be plotted as shown in figure 5, highlighting the gap between what we deliver and what the business wants.

	Performance criterion	Current level	Desired level (required by stakeholders / users)
Product	Suitability of applications	6	8
	Reliability	7	8
	Security	8	8
Process	Project management	7	9
	User support	6	8
	Operational excellence	8	9
People	Friendliness of staff	7	8
	Expertise	7	8
	Business awareness	5	8
Price	Return on investment for projects	6	8
	Operational budget	7	9

TABLE 1. EXAMPLE OF PERFORMANCE CRITERIA
FOR THE STRATEGIC CANVASS

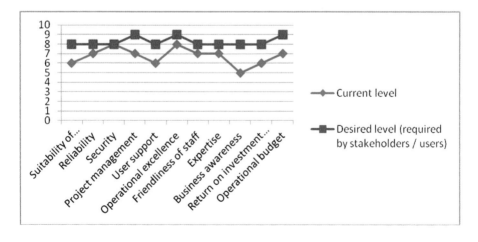

FIGURE 5. A GRAPH SHOWING RELATIVE
PERFORMANCE ON THE STRATEGIC CANVASS

This current situation analysis forms a good basis for analyzing at a high level how the IT department might focus its efforts going forward.

1.5.3 PESTEL

PESTEL analysis is a general analysis looking into the external factors relevant to your strategic plan. It is a six-letter acronym representing the six major external aspects, namely Political, Economic, Social, Technical, Environmental, and Legislative factors.

Areas of influence	Outline of key issues	Possible opportunities	Possible trends
Political	How the political climate might affect IT, not just international or national politics but also politics within your own organization	Opportunities might be to work in new countries, exit countries that are politically unsuitable, or on a local level, look at projects that would be of particular relevance to the senior executive	Trends might include changes in political climates in previously unstable countries. Think about changing political currents in your organization and how this might impact IT.
Economic	Trends in local, national and international economics and how they might affect the implementation and operation of IT	Countries that are showing economic growth ahead of others. From an IT perspective, the focus is usually on currently on delivering better value for money.	Countries emerging from recession, different customer spending profiles. Top level strategy should give an indication for IT to align to.
Social	How the way society behaves in day to day and on-line activities	Think about social media and its relevance for improved productivity, job satisfaction and bringing people together. Also look at the negative side where it may be detracting for performance.	A trend that has been in place for many years, social networking will continue to change, to deliver higher levels of social interaction, better suited to personal and job satisfaction
Technological	The evolution of technology and how it will change the way we do business	Refer to the section on innovation to see how to develop your own view of how technology will change your own business	Trends are around increased networking, erosion of international boundaries, faster performance, SaaS and so on.
Environmental	How we need to consider the importance of the environment around us. Most recent trends in this area have been around green IT.	Improvements in sustainability and becoming 'greener' are vital for the future but need to be done in line with corporate strategy and energy	Green data centres, reduced power consumption, lowering carbon footprints (for example by reducing travel with better video conferencing)
Legislative	Understand key legislation that may affect your business from a technology point of view	This has included Sarbanes Oxley for example in the past, data protection etc.	Examples to think about might be health and safety, data protection, employment etc.

TABLE 2. PESTEL ANALYSIS

1.5.4 SWOT analysis

SWOT analysis is a well-known business tool and is useful for bringing together all the different ideas from the previous analyses. SWOT stands for strengths, weaknesses, opportunities, and threats. The idea is that you play to your strengths, look to overcome your weaknesses, take advantage of new opportunities, and have a plan in place to mitigate the effect of any threats.

STRENGTHS	WEAKNESSES
What is the organization really good at – in the eyes of the customer and relative to the competition	What needs to be improved – in the eyes of the customer and relative to the best competition
OPPORTUNITIES What could improve business performance, looking at new markets, technology, social, political and economic trends	THREATS What could damage sales in the future – looking at new competitors, substitutes and existing competitors as well as other influences

FIGURE 6. OUTLINE OF OUR IT STRATEGY PROCESS

1.6 IT STRATEGY STEP 2: IT OBJECTIVES AND AREAS OF FOCUS

1.6.1 Setting IT objectives

With the business context understood and an assessment of the current situation completed, the next stage is to define the future position. There are two components to this: a high-level view, typically defined by the high-level mission, vision, and values, and the quantitative view, defined by objectives. With IT strategy it makes more sense to focus your energies on developing the IT objectives. These align with the high-level or corporate objectives where these exist. Set objectives in the four areas of the balanced scorecard (amended slightly for the context of IT) as follows:

1. Users and business sponsors (these correspond to the customer in the original model)

2. Business and IT processes and technology

3. People and organization

4. Financial metrics

   Objectives are typically one of four types:

1. Business objectives where IT activity has a direct impact on achieving them

2. IT objectives that are specific to the IT organization, e.g., improving first-time fix on the service desk

3. Compliance objectives, e.g., to meet a particular standard, such as Sarbanes-Oxley

4. Risk reduction objectives, e.g., to reduce reliance on a particular supplier

An example of a business objective might be to increase the company's online sales presence. Clearly IT will help in this. An example of an IT objective might be to reduce IT support costs by 10 percent. An example of a compliance objective might be to meet security standards or data protection compliance (to an agreed level). Finally, risk reduction might relate to reducing dependence on particular suppliers or an obsolete platform.

It can also be helpful here to make guiding statements as to how the objective might be achieved. These guidelines are called themes and might include a desire to standardize on a particular platform or application. It

might suggest a strategic direction for a sourcing plan. These themes do not need to have objective measures against them but act as a guide in decision making.

Figure 7 shows some examples of a number of the measures used by other IT managers in their strategy.

Users & Business Sponsors
User satisfaction
Call answer time
Response to requests (IMAC's)
Easier to use systems
More integrated
Easier for the customer
Speed of response (user terminal)
Accuracy e.g. Billing, reporting

IT Process & Technology
Project lifecycle time
Number of projects delivered (successfully)
Systems reliability & scalability
Total number of outages (different priorities)
Major incident levels
Number of changes implemented
Number of platforms / architectural changes
Level of security / compliance

IT Team / Management
Skills development
Staff retention
Average salary
Training investment
Teamwork
Utilization
Employee survey
Organizational improvement
Internal to external staff ratio

Financial
Benefit realization
Capital & operational expense
Number of suppliers and contract value
Sourcing / outsource
IT asset / stock levels
Governance & decision making

FIGURE 7. EXAMPLES OF IT OBJECTIVES IN THE BALANCED SCORECARD

All objectives must conform to the SMART criteria:

- Specific
- Measurable
- Achievable
- Realistic
- Timely

Once you have chosen your most important measures, the next stage is to set targets for them. Set your target as an absolute number, as a percentage improvement, or as a comparison with a competitor or group of competitors.

High-level objectives can relate to revenue growth, user satisfaction, better value for money, better staff retention, or improved operational efficiency—but they must be realistic. If they are too aggressive, they will not be supported, or they will require you to take unreasonable risks. Make them too easy, and IT risks becoming complacent, eventually losing the support of its stakeholders. You will instinctively know whether or not your strategy demands bold change, requiring aggressive growth and improved performance. This boldness needs to be expressed in terms of high-level objectives.

It makes sense that you know how you are performing against the metric (its current value); otherwise you will not know how much needs to be done. Objectives can relate to supporting a business objective, an IT objective, risk mitigation, or compliance. Define the outcome, not the means. For example, reengineering the sales process isn't an objective; it's the means to achieve a result. And finally look to set both a baseline and a stretch target for each one.

At this point it is important to take stock of your objectives. Back to the earlier point, if you significantly miss the mark in setting your objectives by either being unrealistic, unambitious, or missing key criteria, your strategy will be flawed. So how can we identify everything that needs to be covered in the plan? One of the best ways is to do a situation analysis using the techniques for the previous chapter on business strategy, namely, strategic canvass and PESTEL, and bring your findings together in the SWOT analysis.

In the SWOT analysis, the strengths and weaknesses are about the situation today. Look carefully for existing problems. Opportunities and threats are about the future taking advantage of new opportunities and countering possible threats. For example, we may have a current problem (i.e., weakness) with staff retention, in which case we would look to set an objective to reduce staff turnover by say 10 percent. To complete the picture, you may also wish to compare your performance with others, through a benchmarking exercise for example. When doing this exercise, make a long list to start with, and then look to combine problems together.

Top-level objectives define what success looks like. Be wary of publishing them to the whole organization too early—you will obviously have to share them with the strategy development team, i.e., your management team and key stakeholders. It is normally better to wait until you have worked through the rest of your strategy, or you run the risk of setting goals that are either too difficult or too easy.

Finally, all IT employees' objectives should have a line of sight to the IT strategy objectives, which in turn should relate to the high-level business objectives. These should also be monitored and reviewed on a regular basis.

1.6.2 Dividing up the puzzle

IT strategy is a massive potential activity and without proper structured thinking can end up being so large and complex that the end never comes into view. To overcome the potential problem of complexity, it is important to segment your strategy into a number of broad areas where you want to deliver results. Each of these areas may have a number of issues, usually similar or related problems, that need resolving. Grouping similar problems together will make your strategy much clearer. There is a great saying that to solve an impossible problem, divide it into two really difficult ones. And so it is with strategy, except we are going to show that you may want to divide it into anything between four and ten segments.

This cannot be stressed enough. If your strategy is clear and understandable, your sponsors will find it much easier to support it. Even if they don't agree with what you propose, making it clear will allow them to highlight the problems so that you can make the necessary changes.

We call these key result areas "domains." They provide the supporting framework for your strategy. Each domain will act as a collecting area for related problems. Sometimes these problems can in turn be translated into objectives, where we describe the desired outcome of resolving the problem. So in essence each domain will have its own independent measures.

Define domains according to where you expect to invest time and deliver specific and significant results. First, domains need to be mutually exclusive. In other words strategic activities are segmented so that different problems are addressed with no overlap or duplication. Second, they need to be collectively exhaustive; in other words all of your problems and the objectives you seek to achieve are contained within one of the domains.

This principle of mutually exclusive and collectively exhaustive is known by its acronym, MECE, pronounced "MeeSee." It is at the heart of the consulting thinking of McKinsey's, one of the world's leading strategy consulting firms. It is also described in more detail in the book *The McKinsey Way*.[10]

Very often domains follow process or departmental lines. So it may be that you want to make particular improvements in the area of customer care or manufacturing, for example. Sometimes a domain can be a process group where you have a number of smaller processes that link together. Often we see managers creating a domain called enterprise systems, which brings together all the company-wide generic systems, such as e-mail, reporting, and document management.

So what is the correct number of domains? Our experience is that between five and ten is common—if you have too few, each one becomes quite complex. Too many increases the analysis overhead, and you get more crossover between different groups.

---

10   *The McKinsey Way*, Ethan Rasiel, published by McGraw Hill

This is an ideal situation, but unfortunately strategy is not a perfect science, and often one problem creeps into different domains as there is a degree of interdependence. A good example is security, where security issues arise in different parts of the IT organization. If this is a particularly significant area, it is better to create a separate security domain and resolve all the issues in one place. If it is not a major issue, address the issues within individual domains.

In summary the activities to complete phase one of the IT strategy process are as follows:

1. Put together a full list of all the objectives you wish to achieve by domain.

2. Consolidate them into typically five to ten high-level objectives and set a baseline target and ideally a stretch target for each one

3. Divide your strategy into domains

4. Allocate objectives from the top level to each domain where possible

5. Cross-check to ensure that all key areas of the strategy are included.

1.7 IT STRATEGY STEP 3: PROJECTS AND ACTIVITIES

To summarize, we have reviewed the business context, assessed current performance, divided our strategy into domains, and created a set of objectives. The next step is to put together the list of projects to meet those objectives. Some of these projects will already be underway, and some new ones will need to be added.

Start by listing all the ongoing projects, and group them into similar categories, perhaps relating to the achievement of an individual goal. For example, if there is an objective to increase sales in a new market requiring new products, updated information systems, and additional sales staff, it can be helpful to group all these activities together. This reinforces the idea that meeting the end objective (increased sales in this case) is a team effort. Make sure the activities within each group are sequenced correctly—for example, only scheduling the new sales training when the product is ready for launch and the IT systems are fully working!

During the development of a strategic plan, a number of high-level corporate initiatives will also be identified. Combine them with ongoing projects to identify the full scale of change activity. Prioritize them so that only the most relevant are selected. By now you know all the high-level initiatives and smaller projects that will go toward achieving each strategic objective. Now is the time to assign a senior sponsor, usually a director, who is responsible for ensuring the necessary initiatives are completed and more importantly that the benefits are realized.

With the long list of large and small projects as well as individual tasks, review which are the highest priorities, based on the strategic priorities of your plan and their operational urgency. Starting with the highest priorities, keep only those that you have the resources to complete, and defer or cancel the others. For some of the lower priority projects underway, it may be quicker to finish than to stop them.

It is amazing what an organization can achieve when it can visualize what needs to be done. It makes sense, therefore, to find a way to represent the plan on one page. The best way to start this is to summarize the key milestones from each of the main groups discussed in the previous paragraph. For each key group of projects, identify a number of key tasks or milestones.

At the end of this process, it makes sense to take stock of where you are. The process we are following for the creation of strategy requires each of the phases to align to each other. So the IT objectives are consistent with the business objectives, and similarly the IT activities need to be consistent with meeting the IT objectives. At a high level, you need to be confident that if you complete all the activities and projects listed, you will meet your objectives. At this time you may draw one of a number of conclusions:

1. Yes, indeed, the projects and activities are right and sufficient to meet the objectives.

2. The projects and activities are not sufficient. In this case you need to identify new and additional projects, or alternatively, recognize that the objectives are not realistic and revise them downward.

3. The projects and activities are more than sufficient. In this case you can either reduce the number of projects and activities, or you may wish to revise your objectives/targets upward.

Next calculate the resources for each of the projects and initiatives, add them up for each domain, and then aggregate them for the whole project. Consider how much the external cost of these activities will be in terms of hardware, software, external consultants, and support fees. Compare these with previous financial budgets, and discuss them with the financial department to understand if they are realistic and acceptable. Often the balance of resourcing and budget needs to be reviewed.

The other important consideration is the sequencing of the main initiatives. It is all too easy to take on too much, with a particular temptation to start everything off at the beginning. It is more efficient to prioritize the important work and start this first. Identify a few key milestones for each initiative (typically four or five per project), and draw up a high-level project plan. It makes sense to use the network diagram format (what used to be called a PERT chart) rather than the Gantt format. The aim of this stage is to determine the key dependencies of the overall project plan. A milestone, for example, that has four or five key dependencies should be considered high-risk, as it will be delayed by a delay in any of these tasks. Projects can be delayed by all sorts of reasons. Give consideration to ensure that every project delivers benefits early and consistently, particularly those scheduled to take several months.

This work will yield one of a couple of potential issues. First of all, it is possible that the benefits gained from meeting the stated objectives are out of line with the available resources and budgeted investment. Second, the initial project plan appears too complex with a high level of associated risk. In this case several options become available:

1. Change the value of the objectives, or the objectives themselves.

2. Change the way the objectives are achieved.

3. Mitigate the risks—reduce either the probability or impact of things going wrong.

4. Reallocate the resources.

5. Review the priority and sequencing of the projects.

Think about your options before you do too much detailed planning. Often organizations get into the habit of solving lots of small problems with tactical solutions. Strategic planning offers a rare opportunity to put more innovative, imaginative, or robust solutions in place. Now is probably a good time to meet with your key stakeholders again. A short time spent here pays dividends for ensuring your plan is realistic. There are several options open, and we discuss some ideas for reviewing them in the next section.

1.8 IT STRATEGY STEP 4: OPTIMIZING THE PLAN

1.8.1 Scenario planning for optimizing strategy

Referring back to one of the things we said right at the beginning, creating a strategy that is "good enough" is easy. Creating one that is very good is not. There are a few key pressure points in the process that will move you from good enough to very good. Now is the time to ask yourself, "Is there a better way to do what I have set out to achieve?"

We work with a number of techniques to undertake this evaluation. The one we describe here is one of the simplest and most effective. It is called scenario planning. You may use it in a slightly different way for your disaster or contingency planning. Scenario planning is a common management technique pioneered and used successfully by Shell in the 1970s. When applying it to your strategic process, you need to identify several plausible scenarios. Each scenario provides an example of a possible, but perhaps slightly extreme, set of business conditions. The aim is to provoke a healthy discussion among the management team as to how the organization would respond to each and to verify if your strategy would cope with such scenarios. Scenarios should be both positive and negative.

First of all, review your strategic IT objectives one at a time. For each one think about the factors that enable this to be achieved. Then think about how the same result might be achieved in different ways. Go on to evaluate how it might be done to achieve a different outcome. For example, how might you achieve the same result quicker, or indeed slower? If your budget has been reduced by 10 percent, how might you go about achieving that? Sometimes changing the sequencing of the projects can help considerably in terms of resourcing, or cost or risk. Finally, think about whether this really is the right objective and how else you might deliver an increase in performance in the same area but by focusing on a different definition of the objective. From this assessment review the different options before firming up the one that best meets the needs of the business.

1.8.2 Assessing risk in your IT strategy

Now is also a good time to carry out a detailed risk assessment to understand the suitability of the strategy. Maintain a summarized risk register to monitor and manage key assumptions.

As each of the projects and their related activities are brought together, a number of important dependencies will be identified. In addition, it often becomes apparent that not all of them can be implemented within the time frame. It is important to identify key risks associated with plans and document them in a central register. Do not list every possible thing that might go wrong, but just the top ten or twenty risks that will most adversely affect the plan. A typical risk register is shown in the diagram below.

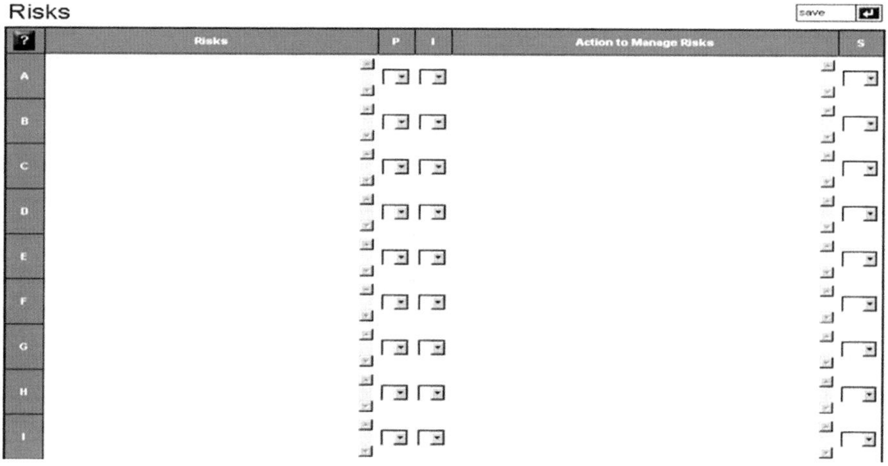

FIGURE 8. AN EXAMPLE OF A RISK REGISTER

There are many different ways to calculate risk, but the most effective when it comes to strategy is to keep it simple. You need to consider two factors: how likely is this risk to happen in practice, and then how serious it would be. To get a figure of merit for how likely the risk is, consider its probability of happening in the strategic time frame, and express this as points out of 10. So if it is only 50 percent probable, score 5 points, and so on. Then measure the severity, where 10 is catastrophic and 0 is no impact. Multiply the probability and the impact together to get an overall score; this gives a score out of 100.

At the end of this stage, the strategic plan is now optimized to deliver its defined objectives.

1.8.3 Is there a better way?

It is easy to think that strategy is an executive exercise that gets in the way of day-to-day operations. Many managers just want to complete their strategy to a standard that meets the approval of their managers. Often the director in charge of reviewing technology strategy is not a technologist. So the blunt truth is that they can only measure the quality of the writing, the color of the graphics, and the confidence of the presentation.

A good strategy holds the key to a successful career for the IT manager. It may take some time for it to be found out, but a poor strategy will soon manifest itself in the form of unfinished projects, high numbers of outages, and poor user satisfaction. It is imperative, therefore, that real consideration is given to finding the best way forward.

Using the principles of innovation we discussed earlier, we need to identify the problem that requires some creative thinking. So the problems you might want to ask yourself are as follows:

1. Is there a way to implement the strategic programs faster?

2. Is there a way to reduce the risk in the strategy, for example by better sequencing of projects so that there aren't too many things changing at the same time, or changing deliverables to provide flexibility to respond to different economic and market conditions?

3. Is there a way to ensure that value is being delivered evenly throughout the strategic time frame, or does it make sense to deliver programs in a different order so more higher-value/higher-priority programs are delivered earlier?

4. Is it possible or worthwhile to delay the strategic programs to take advantage of newer/better/less expensive technology?

5. Is it possible to use resources in a better way, for example, fewer contractors, lower rates, better organization?

6. Is it possible to do it for less money? What are the options in terms of different investment profiles?

Think about other considerations you might want to add. Set some targets, using the scenario planning technique to challenge your thinking. Set 10 percent targets (e.g., how would you deliver the program 10 percent sooner) corresponding with paradigm preserving, as well as, say, 50 percent targets (e.g., what would you really do if the budget was cut in half?) corresponding with paradigm-breaking innovation.

1.9 IT STRATEGY STEP 5: SUMMARIZING YOUR STRATEGY

Strategy is a high-level activity, so it is important to take the time to summarize it concisely. Senior executives find clear, well-thought-out pictures and models much more valuable than long narratives. In this section we present three techniques that you might find useful as part of this communication:

1. Outline project plans

2. Strategic statements

3. Plot on a page

1.9.1 Project plan

One of the most effective tools for communicating strategy is a high-level strategic view of key program tasks and milestones. Bring together each of the groups of projects, and see how they match up to each other. Select the most important milestones, and adjust them so that they are carefully spaced out over the whole year to avoid crisis bottlenecks and the risk of

spreading everyone's attention too thinly. Important milestones include the approval of a business case, completion of the detailed design, the go-live date of a new software application, or the launch of a new product. Sequence these key tasks and milestones so that those delivering more benefit are done first. Even if there is some delay, the organization will still see some benefit. Another tip is to make sure that large projects are structured to deliver benefit in stages (like stepping stones across a river), not just at the end (like trying to leap across the river at once). As a guideline a project should be delivering business benefit at least every three months. The stepping stone approach gives much more flexibility to adjust to changing business conditions; they provide natural points to take stock, pause the project, or amend functionality.

Map out the milestones on a large chart before they are formalized. Start by marking out the next two years on a large sheet of paper, say A2 or A1. Write each milestone on a sticky note, and place it where you think it should be complete. You can then decide which activities need to be moved up in order of priority and which ones can be delayed. Look to see if too many tasks are completing at the same time as this might suggest that there is a higher risk of delay. For large multidivisional organizations, this can be a complex task and may require a more formal approach with key members working together to understand the global outline. Once you have this prototype chart, you can draw it up and print it on A3 or similar.

Figure 9, below, is an example of a strategic project plan drawn in a pictorial way. The individual tasks are joined together in the middle using a "network diagram" format, with a summary timeline at the top. The tasks themselves are merely shown to illustrate the shape of the diagram and do not represent an actual plan.

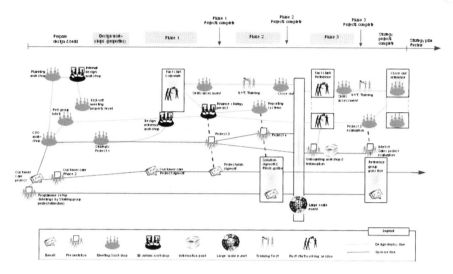

FIGURE 9. AN EXAMPLE OF A SUMMARIZED
(STRATEGIC) PROJECT PLAN

1.9.2 Strategic statements

A strategic statement is a very simple concept. It is a single sentence
that describes a specific objective and summarizes how it is going to be
achieved. Earlier we said that it was important at the beginning of the
strategic plan to separate the objective from the means. In other words,
keep your options open as to how you might achieve a particular goal.
Now that we have now worked through the different options and done
the analysis, we should be confident that we have the right (or best) solution to meet that objective. A strategic statement allows us to state it in
simple terms.

A strategic statement can be one of the following:

- A single solution to meet a specific objective, e.g., We will implement SAP across our Middle Eastern operations to provide common
  reporting across the whole organization (it is recommended that all
  major projects have their own strategic statements).

- A broad solution to meet several objectives, e.g., All new and exist-ing technology platforms will be consolidated into our primary and back-up data centers within two years to reduce support costs and operational overheads and increase system resilience.

- A theme or principle to provide general guidance, e.g., All IT projects will be assigned within the eight high-level programs.

It should be possible to summarize your strategy in about ten sentences.

1.9.3 Plot on a page

The concept of summarizing a strategy onto just one page is very power-ful. When the excitement of the IT strategy has waned in the organiza-tion, what will everyone remember? The answer is, assuming you create one, the "plot on a page." It offers an opportunity to bring out your creative skills to summarize your strategy in an innovative and interesting way. It is normally best to create it on a sheet of A3 or even A2. There are no hard and fast rules as to what to include or how to draw it. The template shown in figure 11 is just one example.

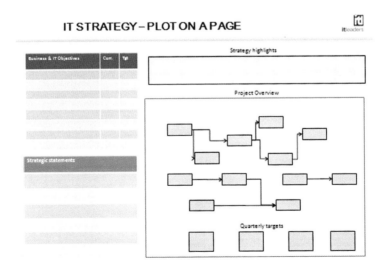

FIGURE 10. AN EXAMPLE OF A PLOT ON A PAGE

Figure 10 lists the business and IT objectives on the left-hand side, with the strategic statements below. The key activities are then shown on the right-hand side using a project network format, with a summary of the plan highlights above. The example above is just one idea. Some companies use it to summarize a before-and-after architecture; some include pictures, graphics, and charts. There are no limits, except that it fits on one page!

1.10 IT STRATEGY STEP 6: COMMUNICATION AND GOVERNANCE

1.10.1 The communication plan

The main activities in this stage to develop and implement an overall communications plan are as follows:

1. Create a communications plan addressing the needs of shareholders, managers, employees, and external partners

2. Identify the most appropriate communication medium, for example, round table discussions, town-hall-type presentations, or one-on-one meetings

3. Prepare the collateral materials for all presentations and communications

4. Once the options have been reviewed and the strategic choice made, the key aspects of the strategy can be confirmed. In summary, this will include the following:

    a. The objectives and targets

    b. The work to be undertaken—prioritized activities and projects

    c. The allocation of resources

d. The sequencing of the projects

e. The investment and budget

Some organizations use a slide presentation format; some organizations use a document (report) format. Whichever format you use, tailor all strategic documents to the audience. The communication plan describes which documents are presented to whom and when. Table 3, below, gives a typical example:

Who to	What	How	Frequency	Owner
Board	2-5 pager	Board meeting	Quarterly	CIO
IT mgt team	20 pager	Team meeting	Quarterly	CIO
IT team	20 pager	Town hall	2 x p.a.	IT mgt team
Key business owners	20 pager	One to one meeting	2 x p.a. (high level)	IT Business managers
Rest of business	20 pager	Internet Email	Quarterly update	CIO

TABLE 3. AN EXAMPLE OF A COMMUNICATIONS PLAN

Finally, remember that the IT strategy is a living document. Review it on a (semi) regular basis. In order to achieve good alignment with the business, it is important to recognize that as the business priorities change, so should the IT strategy.

No two companies communicate in the same way, but in my experience, the following four examples are the most common ways for companies to communicate to the organization.

1. A presentation of the high-level plan to all senior managers. This can act as a run-through or template for them so that they are fully aligned when presenting to the rest of the organization.

2. A town-hall-type meeting to present the high-level strategy to the wider organization. The priorities here are to keep the

presentation short and high-level and also motivational wherever possible.

3. One-to-one meetings may be necessary if some employees are particularly affected by some of the aspects of the strategy.

4. A document that describes the strategy in more detail. Send it to the employees individually. Do not expect that a document posted to the company intranet or internal website will be seen, let alone read, by all employees.

A new strategy will often require significant change from an organization and its people, and the management team must pay particular attention to the change leadership considerations. This will ensure that people not only understand what is going on but also actively support and embrace the change. The key is to make sure that the presentation shows people what is in it for them, their team, and the organization if they implement the change successfully.

In some cases where employees work remotely or across international borders, it is more difficult for everyone to get together in the same place. In this situation, special consideration needs to be given to communication, for example via videoconference or off-site conferences.

1.10.2 An example strategy presentation

The debate as to the correct format for the final IT strategy has been raging forever. The plain truth is that it does not matter. Professional services firms, for example, such as solicitors, accountants, etc., still prefer a narrative. Others prefer a PowerPoint slide presentation. Either way, the following outline may prove useful. It has been used successfully with several organizations.

Business objectives and targets	IT objectives & targets	Strategic statements & themes	Initiatives by strategic Domain
Program benefits	Strategic program plan	Physical architecture (before and after)	Functional architecture (before and after)
Staffing resources	Leadership and Organization	Budgets (capex & opex)	Governance

FIGURE 11. AN EXAMPLE OF TWELVE KEY SLIDES
FOR THE STRATEGY PRESENTATION

It basically lists the key subjects from left to right. So the first topics are the business and IT objectives, following by the strategic statements. Next are the activities and the summarized project/program plan. This is followed by some of the plan detail:

1. Physical architecture (high-level)

2. Functional architecture (high-level)

3. Staffing

4. Leadership structures and organization

5. Investment (capex) and operational (opex) budgets

The final section is the one on governance. This structure can be used as an effective sequence to present the IT strategy to the senior executive. The main purpose of the governance slide is to gain confirmation and commitment from the senior management of their roles and duties in the successful implementation and monitoring of progress.

1.10.3 Presenting to a senior audience

The science of communication has identified that different people respond better to some styles of presentation than others. Nowhere is this truer than in the boardroom. Although not all board members will have the same profile, it is important that the dominant style is used, or you risk losing their interest and hence their support.

Instinctively, more than 60 percent of IT people tend to use a logical and structured style. This is called deductive reasoning and goes something like this:

FIGURE 12. THE LOGIC IN A DEDUCTIVE PRESENTATION

This is all well and good, but unfortunately the majority of senior managers do not care for this style. They prefer a top-down approach. "Give me the highlights," as it were. This approach is called inductive reasoning and goes something like this:

Induction

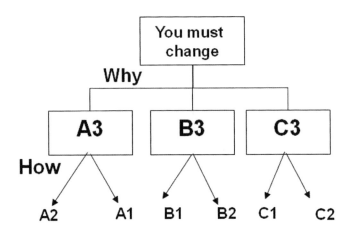

FIGURE 13. THE LOGIC IN AN INDUCTIVE PRESENTATION

Presentations to the senior managers, therefore, should follow this format. Treat it as though you were expecting some of the most important managers to walk out halfway through (which we know happens often enough). If you have used the inductive style for your presentation, you will be OK because you will have started with the key points at the beginning. If you have used the deductive style, explaining all the background first, you won't have reached the main point, and you will have missed your opportunity.

A second point is not to blind your audience with technology, but at the same time, recognize that some of the board members will be very knowledgeable as far as IT is concerned. Similarly, let them learn what they should know or may have forgotten. So, for example, don't patronize them and ask "Do any of you know what the CCBS is?" It's better to say something like, "As you know, the CCBS, our customer care and billing system…"

We also have the following other pointers to help you in the boardroom:

1. Be strategic with a clear message and presentation logic

2. Make visuals clear and concise

3. Brevity is the soul of wit (it is not a speech)

4. Practice, practice, and then practice some more

5. Stay alert—don't start brief and then get verbose

1.10.4 Outline of strategy governance

Monitor and review IT strategy on a regular (typically quarterly) basis to ensure the strategic plan stays relevant and delivers the required results. Specific tasks include the following:

1. Review the strategic objectives and their link to the personal objectives of all IT employees

2. Review the assumptions of the IT strategy, and update it where required

3. Review the IT strategy programs at a high level to ensure that priorities remain valid and benefits are realized (note that this is not the same as the project review meeting)

4. Review the high-level IT strategy risk register

Strategy is an ongoing process rather than something that happens once a year. The strategic plan incorporates all of the major initiatives and subsequently measures their progress and the benefits they deliver.

The senior executive team should meet once a quarter to discuss only strategy and its progress. All aspects should be considered, testing the initial assumptions that the strategy was based on and checking progress

in terms of new products, key IT programs, and operational performance. If you don't have one, help your company set up a central risk register. And in the interim, your monthly routine should also include a catch-up with each of the other key stakeholders.

2. Business Change Leader

2.1 EXCELLENT IT PROJECTS, PROGRAMS, AND CHANGE

ALL IT MANAGERS WILL BE INVOLVED IN PROJECT DELIVERY AT SOME TIME IN THEIR CAREERS. THE INDUSTRY HAS WORKED LONG and hard to promote the successful delivery of projects and to learn from past experience. A number of globally recognized standards have been developed to help with this. If this has somehow passed you by, you will find a quick overview of these (including PRINCE2, PMI, and agile methods) in the last section of this chapter.

Our main concern though is with *excellent IT management* which means moving to the next level in project delivery and may quite possibly involve leading a portfolio of projects. To that end, it is assumed that you are familiar with at least one of these methodologies and are looking for further guidance and practical advice on the successful delivery of projects. IT managers are involved with different complexities of projects, and before we go on, it is helpful to define what is meant by projects, programs, portfolio management, and change leadership:

Project management: A project tends to be linear and temporary, and comprises a set of actions or tasks to implement one computer system or business solution. Because this book is aimed at more senior managers, it offers guidelines for those managers who might be looking after a team of project managers. We also look at project portfolio management, the art of managing progress on a series of projects run by several project managers.

Program management: In contrast, program management tends to be the implementation of a larger change, usually requiring the coordination of several related subprojects to deliver a final result. Senior managers may well be running one program and overseeing the delivery of smaller subprojects into an integrated whole. We look at some of the important techniques for managing these larger-scale programs.

Project Porfolio Management: Project portfolio management is the management of a group of projects. Usually, it is the role of the department head of the project management team, verifying that all the projects run by the team of project managers are on track.

Business change leadership: This is the art of ensuring that a large project or program is fully accepted and adopted by the organization. It is concerned with the people side of implementing a (usually major) business program. It recognizes that such business programs may substantially change the way that individual employees do their work and that this can cause significant anxiety and resistance.

The following diagram shows the relation between projects, programs, portfolio management, and business as usual.

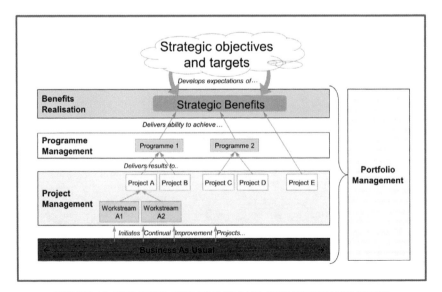

FIGURE 14. PROJECTS AND PROGRAMS (COURTESY IAIN BEGG)

2.2 SUCCESS GUIDELINES 1: GET OFF TO A GOOD START

Our first set of guidelines focuses on the selection of projects themselves and setting a strong foundation for successful project delivery.

2.2.1 Be careful what you ask for

Most business cases that go before the project review committee seem to be really great ideas at the time, only to lose their shine after only a few weeks. And yet most of the reasons that projects go off the rails are entirely predictable at the beginning of the project.

All the more reason to make sure that the project approval decisions are correct. If you are fortunate to be part of the project review process, you should be asking some very tough questions at the outset, and not in a few weeks' time when things aren't going so well. In summary, you should be asking questions in four key areas (see section 3.8 on project portfolio management for more detail):

1. Strategic priorities: if you think that your organization is going to review or change its strategic priorities and that this in turn will materially affect the need for this project, the best advice is to put it on hold

2. The business case: experience tells us that this is the area where most projects are wrongly assessed; make sure you are really clear on the benefits, remembering that some benefits (e.g., direct cost savings) are more easily attainable and more valuable than others (e.g., revenue projections)[11]

3. The ease of project delivery: the resources for the project should be properly sized, taking into account the experience of the project team and allowing for a project contingency (either an allowance in delaying the delivery date, or budget overrun). Additional care

---

11   In chapter 5, we discuss these different types of benefit as part of commercial management, as well as how to calculate business case value.

should be taken at project approval time if adding such a contingency severely reduces the value of the project. This might be the case for a product launch that must be done in time for a critical date, such as a major bank holiday. In addition, the project must meet the needs of the customers and be supported by the business employees, users, and stakeholders alike

4. Durability: ask questions around how long the project will deliver value; in particular, ask if there are new technologies on the horizon that could deliver more value for a fraction of the cost

2.2.2 Choose the right time to start

IT's role in a business project or program is to deliver functionality for business users. And hence the business users must be ready for it. IT managers should be on the lookout for warning signs: key sponsors not turning up to project approval meetings or users being tied up with other operational problems, for example. Speak to key users and sponsors to understand their attitudes about the change. They should be seeing the change as highly positive, an opportunity rather than a burden or a threat. If there are any concerns in this regard, raise it to the project board, and consider postponing the project until the time is right.

CHUCK'S STORY

BACKGROUND

I was working for a utilities company. It had been known for some time that this operating unit was having problems. It frequently appeared on the national news amid stories of poor service quality and very low customer satisfaction. A new management team was brought in to turn things around.

WHAT HAPPENED

The management team was led by a very charismatic figure, an ex–special services officer. Every Wednesday afternoon the management team of eight senior managers met to discuss progress. The meetings were tough, but the chief executive led things forward through a mix of determination and a raw sense of humor.

One afternoon, however, the mood was very different. It transpired that an intruder had held up one of our sales offices at gunpoint. At first we assumed that this was a crazed drug addict. A sales outlet seemed an odd place to choose, though, as we didn't have much cash on the premises. It turned out that this person was in fact one of our customers. He had become so incensed with the level of service we provided that he had been trying for six months to end his contract.

The company was so incompetent that it was unable to carry out this simple task, continuing to send bills and threatening letters for a service that the customer hadn't asked for and didn't want. So frustrated and angry had he become that the only way he could get our undivided attention was at gunpoint.

LESSONS LEARNED

I remember being very shocked at the time, but it did give us a very real sense of what we were doing to our customers. And in turn it did galvanize us to achieve an extraordinary turnaround in the following 18 months. Sometimes it takes an outside event to really make you see things as they really are and force you down a difficult but necessary path.

2.2.3 Choose a good team

Few project managers get to choose the people who are going to work with them. Fortunately, this can be solved by good IT management. If

you are in charge of a number of project managers, an important part of your job is to make sure that the team on each and every project has a balance of skills and experience.

Research by Dr Meredith Belbin identified that project teams should have project members fulfilling each of nine key roles.[12] The Belbin model allows teams to assess their overall structure and identify potential strengths and weaknesses.

Be on the lookout for part-timers, those people who have other responsibilities besides the project itself. For multifunctional projects, such as a company-wide ERP or business intelligence system, the project will need representation from a number of different departments. It is vital, then, that the key project members are committed to the project—and that probably means working full-time on it. Part-timers can be disruptive, turning up as spectators to meetings and too easily able to feign ignorance about issues they should have been responsible for. On the other hand, not unreasonably, full-timers might feel vulnerable at the end of a project, particularly if it is a long one. Organizations need to make sure that successful project members are not rewarded by losing their jobs.

MARK'S STORY

BACKGROUND

At a six thousand-staff global enterprise based in London, a strategic business decision was made to relocate 50 percent of IT and business services roles to a new office in Ireland. The ultimate goal was to reduce the costs of the support services.

---

12   More information on the Belbin roles and project team assessments can be found on their website, www.belbin.com.

Many of the IT roles to be relocated were highly experienced operational staff who typically worked in a highly customized environment. Key to the successful transition of support services was a knowledge transfer to new staff prior to redundancies taking place. The business cost savings were based on a handover of just three months.

WHAT HAPPENED?

Once the business decision was public, it was determined, that the depth of knowledge transfer would require a significant number of dedicated staff. This meant that all current teams were down on head count, and hence services were impacted.

Nonessential work was moved down the priority list (to free up staff for training and knowledge transfer); to do this, governance and resource management was introduced through the transition period to minimize the impact to services. Most new work requests were pushed back, creating a backlog of existing maintenance, all of which would still require resourcing at a later date.

It turned out that three months was not sufficient. A number of redundancies had to be deferred to extend the transition period. This was the result of the incumbent knowledge not simply being of a technical nature, but also based on many years of experience of the systems.

LESSONS LEARNED

- Always fully understand up front the resource requirements to implement such business change.

- Understand the impact on services and costs that such requirements will have.

- Don't underestimate the importance of staff experience. It is not simply a case of recruitment and training.

- Involve trusted IT staff with the deep knowledge to contribute to these calculations.

- Consider the longer term impact of additional pressures on staff and the implications of low morale.

- Ensure that the resulting risks to services are signed off on by the business.

- Communications to the end users are essential so that their expectations are managed.

2.2.4 Be clear on what is being delivered

Projects need to be performed and delivered under certain constraints. Often, when a project is first conceived, it is required "better, faster, cheaper!" Of course, not every project can be delivered immediately for no cost and meet all the quality criteria. These factors are mutually exclusive. The general view is that you can have two of the three:

1. Quickly and to a good standard, but it will be expensive

2. Quickly and cheap, but it will not be very good quality

3. High quality and cheap, but it will take a long time

This is shown in the triangle below. A stakeholder will need to choose where on the triangle the project should fit.

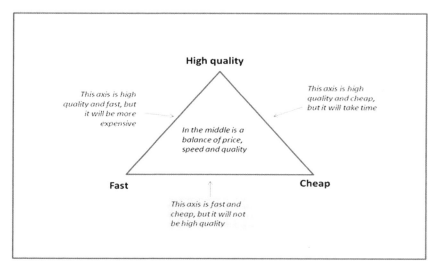

FIGURE 15 - THE TRADE OFF OF COST, SPEED AND QUALITY

The time constraint refers to the amount of time available to complete a project. The cost constraint refers to the budgeted amount available for the project. The scope constraint refers to what must be done to produce the project's end result. These three constraints are often competing: increased scope typically means increased time and increased cost, a tight time constraint could mean increased costs and reduced scope, and a tight budget could mean increased time and reduced scope.

The discipline of project management is about providing the tools and techniques that enable the project team (not just the project manager) to organize their work to meet these constraints.

2.2.5 Create a high-level architecture

Once the business case is approved, the information systems department needs to get down to its work. Before the project gets too far down the track, there should be a proper technical design. IT project members need to get together and agree on what is required and in particular which systems and process changes are needed. From the requirements the team should be able to put together a high-level architecture that describes

what the future technical configuration should look like. The aim of this is threefold:

- First of all, staying at the high level provides a useful mechanism for the architects to identify the best technical solution. Assuming that everyone stays at the high level (and this is a big assumption), it allows the group to think of alternative high-level solutions. The benefit here is that developing a high level (technical) solution, before moving to the detail, means that the detail only needs to be done once.

- Second, drawing up a high-level architecture provides the project team with a view as to how much work is required.

- Finally, it acts as a description of the project "vision." Although vision is normally associated with the business improvement that a project will deliver, a high-level technical picture can also help the project team to visualize the end point.

MICHEL'S STORY

A financial services company based in California was looking to migrate its customer order platform to incorporate additional new services. The technical architects had a very difficult job to do, and the block diagrams were very complex. For each block at the high level, there was a detailed technical specification. Before all the technical specs were finished, the team enhanced the overview block diagram, making it understandable by the rest of the team. This meant that all architects had to agree on this diagram.

This overview schematic shaped the architecture from a strategic point right at the outset. In turn this meant that the detail only had to be done once. The diagram was "colored in," as one of the architects put it, and was suitable to be communicated to the business stakeholders and users. This turned out to be more important than was first imagined. First of all, it was important to the project team that they could understand what the technologists were trying to produce. Second, it helped them to understand that this was not a simple task and required their full attention.

2.3 SUCCESS GUIDELINES 2: MANAGING PROJECT PROGRESS

This book is concerned with managing projects at the higher level, so we focus on techniques for program managers and project portfolio managers.

2.3.1 Develop strong project management skills

If you are running a project team, the importance of having standards and methods around managing the different projects will be no surprise to you. It only takes a few days of trying to consolidate reports in different formats to realize the value of good, consistent reports that can be aggregated to give an overall view. This applies equally whether you are a program manager bringing together the subprojects into an integrated picture or a project portfolio manager required to manage diverse projects.

Section 2.7 gives some guidelines of two leading project methodologies: PRINCE2 and PMI's project processes. The thoughts in this chapter assume you have a good project methodology in place and are constantly striving to get the most out of it.

First, project managers must be trained in the project method used by your organization. When we poll senior managers, the vast majority are using some project methodology in their organizations. Interestingly, almost all of these organizations have adapted a standard framework to suit. If you have modified PRINCE2, for example, and you recruit a qualified PRINCE2 project manager, you may still need to give them a grounding in your particular methods, the report formats, frequency, how you manage risks, and so on.

Second, recognize that fully qualified project managers are no guarantee of successful project delivery. Project management is analogous to driving a car. Just because you have a driver's license does not make you a good driver. It takes experience as well. Figure 16 below shows our model of the key management skills for managing projects. These skills are represented in different forms in the different project methodologies, and many of the key disciplines of project management require advanced people management and analytical skills. As the leader of a project team, you will have a permanent responsibility for identifying problems and developing the skills of your team.

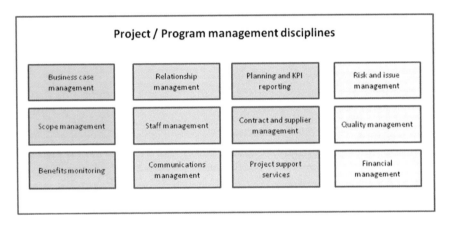

FIGURE 16: PROJECT AND PROGRAM MANAGEMENT DISCIPLINES

There is so much for a project manager to learn about project management techniques that it is difficult to know where to start. Table 4 was put together by senior managers who have attended our leadership courses as a list of top guidelines for project managers to focus on.

GUIDELINES FOR YOUR PROJECT MANAGERS

Make a good plan. A good plan that everyone understands and agrees with is probably the most important advice. The plan

must address the real priorities of what you are trying to achieve and have the necessary resources. There should be enough planning detail for it to be clear what is to be done but not so much that the planning needs to be recast every week. Don't assume that more tasks are better. Anyone can use the copy function in Microsoft Project!

Stay informed. Keep all of your communication routes open, and keep listening to the advice of others. In particular your champions will give you frequent feedback from the field as to how things are going, current issues, and potential future problems. Actively seek the advice of others, and adjust your plans accordingly. Keep everyone updated on progress and milestones that have been achieved.

Stay flexible. There is a helpful phrase used as a watchword in the military: "Indecision is the key to flexibility." It means don't rush to make decisions that you don't need to. A good example is procurement approvals. Your vendors will want you to buy early and in large quantity. Resist this pressure, and buy only what you need when you need it. Staying flexible may mean changing targets or reviewing project deadlines.

Keep to time. Don't delay deadlines unless you have to. It sends the wrong message, and people will use it as an easy way out of project difficulties. I remember interviewing a promising project manager who said he always delivered his projects on time. In reality it turned out that he kept all his project plans on his computer and restricted access to them. And any time things looked like they might slip, he just moved the end dates out. Simple!

Focus on benefits. Stay focused on what you are trying to achieve. Don't get distracted trying to achieve too many things at once. It is like carrying suitcases. It is easy to carry one or two at once. As soon as you try to carry four or five, it becomes impossible. Keep checking that the results are the right ones.

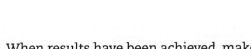

When results have been achieved, make sure that they are recognized by senior management and that the team is properly congratulated and rewarded.

Look after your team all the time, and be on the lookout for how everyone is performing. Keep them all motivated, busy, and working together. Set up regular opportunities to share information, and keep celebrating success. Where possible, be on the lookout for good people who may want to join the project. Good teams attract good people, and good people make good teams.

Don't do everything yourself. To use a musical analogy, it is not possible for one person to play a symphony, however talented they are. Substantial projects need the combined efforts of many players. In any business project, many team members with different skills are needed to create the finished product. Your role is that of the conductor, recognizing and empathizing with what everyone needs to do. Doing the work of your team members (even if you think you are good at it) is highly counterproductive.

Handle conflicts early. As the metaphorical conductor, your job is to ensure that everything works in harmony. As the project progresses and the pressure increases, problems are increasingly likely to appear. Be on a constant lookout for problems, and catch them as early as possible. If there are personal disputes, speak to both parties individually before you bring them together. Telling people to "sort it out" or "just stop it" is an ineffective management approach in today's business world. It is important to identify whether a dispute has arisen out of personal differences or project differences. Seek to understand the basis of the real problem, and take steps to resolve the root cause.

TABLE 4. ESSENTIAL PROJECT GUIDELINES

2.3.2 Make them sweat the small stuff

Project managers are paid to sweat the small stuff. Their project plan needs to contain all the necessary tasks so there are no surprises along the way. Project managers should know where the critical path is and what the key dependencies are.

The most common way to present a list of tasks is the Gantt chart (as opposed to a network diagram or what used to be known as a PERT chart). The Gantt chart has the advantage of listing all the tasks. The duration of the task can be easily seen by the length of the task bar it represents on the Gantt chart.

Gantt charts are not so good at showing dependencies as often the dependency lines merge and overlap. In this case it helps to show a summary of the project in the network format too. The network format can be time-consuming to create but has immense advantages in showing the "shape" of the project and can identify problems that Gantt charts can't. It is highly recommended for project review meetings as it allows managers to quickly see at a high level what is going on with the project.

> **Why projects fail: Don't lose your RAG[13]**
>
> A key principle of successful project management is KISS (Keep It Simple and Straightforward). And in a simple world, using RAG (Red, Amber, Green) reporting, amber or red status means "I need help."

---

13   "Don't lose your RAG," Iain Begg, IMB Consulting. Full paper available at www. imb-consulting.co.uk.

Sphere of influence

The project manager's immediate sphere of influence includes those things that they themselves can fix. A project manager reporting his or her status to the project board should use the amber or red status only for issues that are outside this sphere of influence. Project managers should always have risks and issues to address, but that does not mean the project should be amber or red.

Red versus amber

Some managers don't like projects that suddenly appear as red and think they should first go to amber. Don't be fooled. If your project needs urgent help, the sooner you flag it, the better.

Crying wolf

Project managers should not use amber and red to panic the project board into allocating more resources. Amber and red status should only be for risks and issues outside the project manager's sphere of influence that may affect a successful project outcome.

Don't get angry!

In his book, *How NASA Builds Teams*, Charles Pellerin[14] writes that one of the major failings of the Hubble telescope mission was the behavior of NASA toward its contractors. As one contractor was quoted, "Eventually we were so tired of the beatings, we stopped reporting problems." A sign of a good project board is that problems can be easily raised and discussed without them falling into an argument of blame and retribution.

TABLE 5. DON'T LOSE YOUR RAG

14 *How NASA Builds Teams*, Charles Pellerin

When it comes to detail, work breakdown structures may also help. The work breakdown structure (WBS) is a tree structure that shows a subdivision of effort required to achieve an objective—for example, a program, project, and contract. The WBS may be hardware-, product-, service-, or process-oriented.[15]

A WBS can be developed by starting with the end objective and successively subdividing it into manageable components in terms of size, duration, and responsibility (e.g., systems, subsystems, components, tasks, subtasks, and work packages), which include all steps necessary to achieve the objective.

The work breakdown structure provides a common framework for the natural development of the overall planning and control of a project or program and is the basis for dividing work into definable increments from which the statement of work can be developed and technical, schedule, cost, and labor hour reporting can be established.

2.3.3 Keep a high-level overview for yourself

Rule number one: project reports must be useful and to the point. If you are running a team of project managers, you will be delighted that they are taking care of the detail. Even though the project managers deal with a lot of information, don't let them put the "monkey on your back"[16] by involving you in their detail.

To avoid micromanaging it is all the more important that they provide the right information to assess progress. Have a standard format for project status reports. If you find yourself reading a lot of irrelevant (i.e., not interesting) information, then revise the format. Keep in mind that one size may not fit all. More complex projects require different reporting structures.

---

15   For more information on Work Breakdown Structures, see the Project Management Book of Knowledge (PMBOK), published by the PMI.

16   "Who's got the monkey," Onckon and Wass, *Harvard Business Review* reprint 99609

STEPHEN'S STORY (PART 1): IMPLEMENTING A MOBILE PHONE NETWORK

Where a detailed project plan is important for smaller projects, a high-level view is essential for larger programs. Some years ago I worked for a major telecommunications company that was building a mobile network in France. There were about fifty major projects within the overall program. Each project plan had hundreds of project tasks. It was even more important then to see how the overall program was developing without getting sucked into the detail.

We created a high-level view using a network diagram format printed on A1 with about two hundred key milestones. It was easy to visualize how the program would pan out—a bit like looking at a time-lapse-type view of the future. Each milestone probably represented about $2 million of capital spend on average. It proved a vital tool to see how progress was being made and how the major projects within the overall program were interacting.

When it comes to reviewing project reports, take a look at the risk register that is presented. Good project managers should be able to identify and report just the top five to eight risks from the full risk register. Conversely, a project that is not being managed well can often be spotted by the fact that the project manager either reports all the risks, suggesting that he or she has no understanding of the relative importance of each one, or none at all.

2.3.4 Managing costs, contracts, and suppliers

Project managers need to keep a tight rein on budgets. This usually means keeping a tight rein on suppliers, be they contractors or technology specialists, systems integrators, equipment suppliers, or developers.

One of the key lessons from our research and delegate feedback is to get the timing of purchasing right. It is better to approve purchases for delivery slightly ahead of when they are needed and avoid buying in large quantities until absolutely necessary. Set up project costs codes for each project, and manage supplier approvals carefully. Strike a good balance between putting the right checks in place to keep costs under control and slowing down project progress.

Give yourself as much time as possible when signing up vendor services to agree on contract terms. Include clauses that protect you from vendor problems with implementation and subsequent support. If a vendor senses that time is not on your side, they may use it to their advantage, persuading you to take on services before the contracts are fully signed. While there may be times when this is the only course of action, the recommendation is to start work on contracts at the earliest opportunity, make sure there is a team dedicated to the task, and keep competitive tension in the deal as long as possible.

WES'S STORY: TELEPHONY AND CONTACT CENTER SYSTEM

BACKGROUND

The organization that I work for has three sites with call centers at two of them handling almost 1 million calls per annum. Both had different telephone systems that were old and expensive to support. My department was tasked with identifying what benefits might be available from a replacement phone and contact system, building a business case, selecting a supplier, and then managing the subsequent implementation.

WHAT HAPPENED

The project kicked off, and all project team staff signed up to a project charter that had commitments around project governance and communication. This worked extremely well as all staff knew what was expected of them. We also utilized a web-based project management and collaboration system for the first time. This enabled the project team, including external staff, to monitor the progress of all tasks as well as collaborate and share information. This created a more productive, well-informed project team. It also enabled me as project manager to have up-to-date information on all project tasks at all times, which, needless to say, aided decision making and resulted in fewer surprises.

The project sponsorship was strong, supportive, and trusting, expecting that any issues would be reported as they occurred. This, together with close project management, enabled the project to be delivered on time, on budget, and within a tight time scale.

LESSONS LEARNED

While the project was a success, we learned a number of lessons, both good and bad, from this project. It was certainly a positive to set up a project charter as everyone knew what was expected of them and this made them more productive project team members. The use of a web-based project management system worked extremely well for the staff in my organization. However, it was not available to the delivery partner prior to placing the order, and it was less efficient at managing their tasks. This was also one of the first projects where we introduced a robust benefits realization tracking process. So far, I'm pleased to say, they are currently on track.

High-quality suppliers can often help enormously with expertise, insights, and guidance on what is working and what isn't. Resist the temptation to confine them to the basement. Like any high-quality professional, they will work much better with a good working environment. Provide them with access to office facilities where they need it, but, at the same time, don't feel obliged to set aside free office space if they are not working full-time on the project.

2.3.5 Set up good project governance

Project governance does not have to be difficult. In IT organizations project governance usually works at three levels. First there is the project review meeting. This is the (typically weekly) review of project progress with the main project members and stakeholders. Depending on the size of the project (and particularly with programs), there may be sub meetings that feed their findings into the project review meeting. Second, there is the IT project review meeting. This is normally run by the IT director or head of IT projects. This meeting verifies that the IT project teams are fulfilling their obligations in the delivery of the project. The chairman can then take the findings from this meeting into the higher-level project governance board.

The project governance board is where all company projects are reviewed. These meetings review the progress of capital investment decisions. They are therefore extremely important, yet a surprising number of organizations do not have formal governance at this level. If your organization is one of these, you may wish to consider working with your senior management to set it up. The importance of this (organization-wide) high-level project review is discussed in book four in this series in the section on governance.

Project review meetings are important for many reasons; obviously they read out the progress of the project and highlight issues that may require management decisions. But they also showcase the ability of the

project teams and, in particular, the project manager. Since the meetings are important, the project team leader should spend time with his or her project managers ahead of time to prepare them and make sure they keep to the point.

Avoiding Project Sponsorship Becoming a Spectator Sport: Our Top Three Tips[17]

Projects don't fail in the end; they fail in the beginning. Project governance is the most common reason projects fail. The following three tips will help you to set your project up for success (for more on project sponsorship, go to www.imb-consulting.co.uk).

1. Goal setting

If you were to ask the project manager and project sponsor, "What are the goals of this project?" nine times out of ten, you will get a different answer. The reason could be a lack of communication, different assumptions, or the fact that time has moved on and the priorities have changed. Together the project sponsor and project manager should put together a mission statement that encapsulates the project's goals and success criteria. Review this periodically as the project progresses.

2. Give airtime to the project manager

The responsibility of the project sponsor includes articulating the high-level scope (i.e., goals and success factors), approving the proposed solution, securing financial and human resources, making prioritization decisions, and exerting his or her power to facilitate the resolution of issues and risks. An experienced and

---

17   "Avoiding Project Sponsorship becoming a spectator sport," Iain Begg, IMB Consulting. Full paper available at www.imb-consulting.co.uk.

hard-nosed project manager would be expected to provide delivery-focused plans, identify issues and potential solutions, mitigate risks, and prioritize to meet deadlines. Without the two speaking regularly to each other, the project sponsor and project manager are likely to make assumptions that may pose significant risk to the successful delivery of the project.

3. Getting the governance right

A project will consist of (in descending order of importance) the business sponsor, the project steering group or project board, stakeholders, affected parties, and interested parties. It is important to identify which category project members fall into to get the best results for your project. Some stakeholders are incentivized to see a project succeed and will move heaven and earth to make it so. But not all stakeholders can commit to attend steering committee meetings, so a small (highly motivated) subset should be elected as the decision makers to form the project board.

TABLE 6. AVOID BECOMING A SPECTATOR SPORT

Project review meetings should be less about project progress and more about making key decisions. If something has gone wrong, the project team leader should work with the project manager prior to the meeting to discuss the strategy. Similarly, if a particularly difficult stakeholder is expected at the meeting, the project manager should meet him or her ahead of time (with the team leader if necessary) so that any disagreement doesn't hold the meeting hostage. Project managers should choose their attendees carefully so meetings don't become too big and unmanageable.

2.3.6 Communicate clearly to all parties

Good communication between management and employees is vital in all successful change programs. Communication needs to be open, working across different levels of seniority and regardless of position, offering an openness in discussing program issues. There needs to be a free flow of information, ensuring that team members have access to what they need to know in order to achieve their objectives. There should be regular formal communication as well as the smart use of informal channels.

JOHN'S STORY: THE NEED FOR BUY-IN

BACKGROUND

Every project manager talks about the need for communication and buy-in. Of course this means different things to different people. A client of ours told me a story of a large project that they were working on. It required a massive upgrade of the technology platform to enable the launch of a range of new services.

WHAT HAPPENED

It was so urgent that the former technology officer had awarded the project management contract to a company that had recently worked on a successful product launch. But the project was starting to stall. It soon became clear that the project management company was unqualified to deal with such a complex technical launch. The project was estimated to take nine months, and three months into the project, the completion date was still nine months away.

An old saying came to mind when I was told this story. "We never have enough time to do things properly but often find the time to do things twice." And so it was in this case. Soon the project management contract had been rewarded to a major international systems integrator, and we started again from scratch.

The systems integrator put in their elite program management team and technology experts. Within a matter of days, it was evident that things were starting to move forward, even though the project was effectively still three months behind schedule. It was now March, and the original date for product launch was September. To be honest, most people in the company were expecting completion toward the end of the year.

The new project team worked closely with the key business sponsors, and in July, just five months later, the projected launch date was predicted to be somewhere toward the end of September. The new CIO was speaking to the head of customer operations discussing what he thought was good news.

The head of customer operations said that while she was impressed with the progress that the IT department had made on the project, she was getting some resistance from the sales force. That morning she had received a petition with one hundred signatories asking for the launch date to be delayed.

The CIO was furious. He could not understand why the sales force, whose only obligation was to attend a four-hour training course, would not be ready when his team had spent sixteen hours a day in the last six months trying to get things finished.

LESSONS LEARNED

The lesson learned was basically that even though the program managers, the IT department, and the key business sponsors were all fully aware of the stellar progress of the project, no one had bothered to tell the salespeople that things were back on track. They were still expecting a launch date toward the end of the year.

As the case study above describes, communication is not just talking to those people who will be turning up to the status meetings. It is about telling everyone who will be affected and making sure they are prepared well in advance for the change. Stakeholders exist throughout the organization. Apart from the project team itself, they include the following:

1. Key business specialists

2. Senior management and sponsors

3. All the managers whose departments are affected by the change (including IT departments such as IT operations)

4. All users who will have to adopt the new systems

A plan should be in place for how the project will communicate to each of these stakeholder groups in turn. Remember that the same method of communication will not work for the different groups. If you are providing training programs, monitor the course quality, and put critical tests in place to verify that the training has been completed and is fully understood.

2.3.7 Keep measuring value (SPRINT)

One of the dangers of project management is that delivering the project plan successfully does not always translate into a successful project. Market conditions may change, for example, between a project starting and a project completing. It is worthwhile to keep monitoring the value your project delivers, and to this end it is helpful to have a checklist to help. The one we recommend is called SPRINT, which stands for Situation, Problem (or opportunity), Risks, Impact, Needs, and Timing. The SPRINT tool suggests that you make a simple one-line statement on each of the six items and regularly review them.

1. Situation: This is the business driver that caused your project to be set up in the first place. The situation is similar to the business con-

text and describes the market opportunity in the case of a business project.

2. Problem (or opportunity): What is the problem that the business faces, or what opportunities is it looking to exploit? Create a statement that summarizes the specific problem that the project is seeking to address.

3. Risks: What are the risks of not doing the project, what are the downsides of doing the project, and what are the significant things that may go wrong? This is not intended as a detailed risk assessment at this time.

4. Impact: What is the benefit that is expected from the project? It is important to keep reviewing this.

5. Need: What are the key features that are needed by the project to ensure that the value is delivered, and are they being delivered?

6. Timing: How quickly does the project need to be completed based on assessments of the market competition? It is clear that if competitive offerings are launched that impact the value of the project, the project may need to be delivered faster. Similarly, if the market demand fades, it might be worth putting a project on hold

We have come across many companies with ambitious projects and change programs. Some of them are successful and others less so. One of the biggest problems with the less successful organizations is that they confuse unrealistic targets with ambition. All companies strive to stay ahead of their competition. But any change program has to be realistic, and in our opinion one of the best ways to achieve this is to deliver value in stages.

In our project management courses, we talk about the importance of stepping stones. These are almost like points of safety along the route of

the project plan. These save the project manager from having to deliver everything at once, analogous to making one enormous leap from one riverbank to the other. The stepping stone approach means that you break the project down into sequential phases. The project can then be appraised at various points along the path and the course changed if required.

One of the options might be to change the project deliverables, and one might be to delay the project. The most common reason for project delay is a scarcity of resources, particularly on the end user side. But there may be other reasons, such as changing economic conditions or reprioritization of projects.

STEPHEN'S STORY (2): KEEP DELIVERING VALUE

BACKGROUND

When a French mobile telephone provider won its license to build a GSM network in France, it embarked on a long project to build the central switches, radio subsystems, and transmission. Notwithstanding the fact that the license bid itself took over six months, building a competitive network requires huge skill and dedication over many months.

There was a danger that the organization would lose energy. Huge amounts of work had been done, but it sometimes seemed difficult to keep the end goal in sight. It was for this reason that when the central infrastructure was in place, including the main switches and primary radio network, the company chose as its next project to get the offices connected and working.

This meant that employees of the fledgling mobile operator could see for the first time what they were trying to create. They were able to make phone calls using new handsets on their own network.

LESSONS LEARNED

It would still be several months before the secondary radio network was in place and the company was ready to launch. But
this first victory was a very valuable step in the company's his-
tory. The management team was reminded of the importance
of delivering small successes along the path.

2.3.8 The art of managing project portfolios

Any manager in charge of other project managers needs to be able to
review all of the projects in their responsibility. This process of managing
and reviewing a collection of projects is called project portfolio management. Indeed, in large global organizations there are generally multiple
portfolios, e.g., functional portfolios and regional portfolios, which will
often compete for resources and for priority.

If you are on a project review team, you may have encountered a
number of frustrations, which would be very typical of this type of meeting. Project review meetings can often be drawn out, with project managers talking at length about the projects they are close to. To preserve
everyone's sanity, it is important to maintain some discipline. Project
managers should get into the habit of summarizing their projects and
project status in two minutes. This prevents them from "winging it" and
using the project review meeting as their time to prepare!

Effective governance of a project portfolio also means dealing a firm
hand in reviewing priorities. All too often organizations approve projects in one business context and fail to review them when the context
changes. There are many things that can change the context:

1.   The economic market conditions

2.   The business case and the business priorities

3. The cost or time scale of the project

4. The impact of other projects

On the final point, there is sometimes a view that if a project has been approved, it must be done as soon as possible and at all costs. This is a false assumption. Every project takes up resources—resources that are not then available to other projects. Just because a project underway has a good business case does not mean there aren't better ones. Effective project portfolio managers have an instinct and an understanding of which projects stand in the way of more valuable ones.

IT managers should not object when the business wishes to change priorities. On the contrary, this should be welcomed. It is a fact that top-caliber managers are more comfortable in changing priorities, putting projects on hold, and canceling them than less experienced ones.

On the other hand, it is not healthy for projects to be constantly started and stopped. What is needed is a rational way to evaluate projects that allows the business to focus IT project teams on their priorities. The best way to do this is with a project portfolio management tool. There are many on the market, but we offer the following four guidelines for successful IT portfolio management:

1. Light in weight: a key benefit of project portfolio management is that the whole business uses it

2. Describes the value of the project in business terms, not IT terms

3. Provides sufficient detail for the business and IT to identify and mitigate risk jointly

4. Acts as the primary vehicle to measure benefits (and value for money)

Even without the tool in place, it is still important to measure the relative importance of different projects.

We have developed a four-point guideline that we call A to E. A stands for "Alignment index"—this is the overall measure that we will use to measure the value of a particular project. The alignment index comes from the makeup of four metrics:

B: Is this project a *business* priority given the current situation and strategy?

C: Is this project *cost-effective*, providing robust benefits for a good price?

D: Is this project *deliverable* given time and resource constraints?

E: Will the value *endure* beyond project completion?

The B and C components are more important than D and E. Some companies, therefore, double the value of B and C to give a more accurate weighted measure. However, much of the value of this technique is around the discussion of projects rather than any precise value.

	Title	B	C	D	E	A Score	Action	Comment
1	Project A	10	8	9	9	90%	Go	Significantly increases market share
2	Project B	9	9	4	8	75%	Modify	Good project but must reduce cost
3	....	10	7	8		73%	No Go	Has only a short term impact
4	....	9	9	9	7	85%	Go	Creates significant brand awareness
5	....	9		9	7	68%	No Go	Not acceptable to key stakeholder
6	....	4	3	10	3	50%	No Go	Non starter

FIGURE 17. PROJECT ALIGNMENT INDEX

The aggregate "A score" of a project (column 7 in table 3 above) does of course change throughout its lifetime. This may be caused by the following:

1. The business priority changing because the business strategy is revised

2. The cost-effectiveness (i.e., business case) changing because market forecasts change or project costs increase

3. The deliverability changing because of problems with resourcing or the supplier

4. The useful life of the project changing (its durability) as new technologies are announced the supersede the existing one

For this reason, therefore, projects should be continually reviewed to see if they are still well aligned to the business priorities. And if they aren't, it is important to act quickly. Clearly it rarely makes sense to stop a project if it is close to completion. However, as we have observed, it is the more successful managers who are much more willing to stop projects that are not delivering.

2.3.8.1 IT project portfolio meetings

To the head of IT projects, the project portfolio meeting is a vital tool in managing the performance of project delivery in the organization, providing an opportunity for IT project managers to come together and share experiences. If the chairman does not exercise discipline, these meetings can be incredibly tedious. It helps of course to have a sharp project reporting format. The project readout too should be short and sharp, leaving time for the head of IT projects to ask some more incisive questions. In table 7 we list some of the questions that may help you assess true project progress and status. The sharp-eyed reader will infer that not all project statuses are accurate. And they would be dead right!

Questions to Ask at Project Portfolio Review Time	
What can I do to help?	A good question—this always puts project managers on their guard the first time they are asked! (Don't ask it, though, if you are not prepared to help.)
What are the biggest risks and how have they been derived?	The idea of the question is twofold. First of all, it will tell you if the project manager has considered the risks, and second, whether he or she has a view as to which ones they should work on.
How good are the estimates (e.g., of project plans, task lengths, budgets, etc.)?	A tricky question because they are estimates. Usually the project manager will talk about something else, and, if you listen carefully, you will find out what he or she is concerned about.
What have been the specific project achievements in the last week?	This is quite an aggressive question, but one to ask if you think your project manager has either been busy on other things or is not focused.
Did you do what you said you were going to do?	This is a telling question. It is easy to list achievements but harder to admit that we didn't quite achieve what we set out to do.

On a scale of one to ten, how happy are you with the project?	This is a bit of a trick question. Good project managers will never give a project ten out of ten as they are always looking for improvements—and they also know that if they say everything is great, then resources may be handed out elsewhere. Ten out of ten suggests a project manager who sees the world through rose-tinted glasses and is therefore more likely to get caught out by "unexpected" problems.

TABLE 7. PORTFOLIO REVIEW QUESTIONS

2.4 SUCCESS GUIDELINES 3: CLOSING THE PROJECT

Any project team manager must be there for the team. And the time he or she is most needed is often as the project is nearing completion. It is all too easy for project managers and project teams to take their eye off the ball, trying to secure a role on another project that is about to kick off. But experience tells us that there are many things that can go wrong on a project right at the end.

2.4.1 Get ready early for the "go-live"

As a project nears its close, attention moves toward the operational mode. Most operational managers will tell you that this is often too late. Certainly experienced project organizations ensure that operational managers are involved in the project from the earliest stages so that the problems of performance, scalability, systems management, security, and so on are properly considered.

Training courses should be completed by all users who will be using the system. User manuals, including quick-start guidelines, should be

created and distributed to all users. The application support teams need to be fully trained on the new system (assuming there are software support implications), and there should be enough personnel to field calls on go-live. It may be worth considering a special "media-style" campaign, using the intranet, company newsletter, posters, etc. to inform everyone of the changes being planned and the go-live date.

JOHN'S STORY

BACKGROUND

A utilities company in Houston, Texas was looking to implement a major change program. The company had grown quickly through acquisition and was now comprised of five separate divisions. The head office believed that the future lay in standardized information systems to realize the economies of scale of the acquisitions. The head office CIO department was proposing an integrated solution using best-in-class software applications, integrated with an Enterprise Architecture Integration (EAI) layer. However, unfortunately, the biggest division already had its own custom-developed system, which it was unwilling to relinquish.

WHAT HAPPENED

Fortunately, two of the divisions had already signed up, and within four months, the first of them had gone live and quickly started to realize benefits. The implementation team realized that the project had gained significant momentum and still did not want to give up on the biggest division. The central CIO team was also smart enough to realize that it could not impose a new system on anyone that was unwilling to implement it.

Instead the CIO spent significant time with the reluctant operating division, in particular with the main business directors, asking them to talk about the problems they were encountering. It soon became apparent that all was not well with their bespoke system. Some elements that had been developed recently were operating well, but the older modules were starting to become slow and cumbersome.

Rather than try to persuade this division to move to the new system in one go, the CIO decided to approach the implementation in a step-by-step way. The division agreed to replace their oldest module, which had the biggest problems, with its equivalent from the new architecture. Gradually, when the operating division came to see the benefits of the new module, they asked for the implementation of the other modules to be accelerated. The project was completed within twenty-four months, almost the same time it would have taken if they had tried to do everything at once.

LESSONS LEARNED

There were several lessons to take from this. The first came down to trust. The operating division did not believe that a so-called off-the-shelf system could provide the depth of functionality that was needed. It turned out that this wasn't the case. But, by not forcing the issue, the head office allowed the local operation to identify problems themselves and take ownership of resolving them.

The second lesson was about not giving up. It was important for the head office to continue the momentum of the overall change project. It was not the CIO's intention to replace everything as quickly as it turned out but rather to take things a step at a time. The step-by-step approach did give the operating unit time to adjust to the change, and once the project had started, there was no going back.

2.4.2 Make the change "irreversible"

Going through a major change program is tough. The program itself is the just the end of the beginning. It is vital that any new system is accepted by the users—good training helps, but users also have to be committed in their hearts and minds, and that is down to strong leadership from the business. IT managers need to coach, guide, and support this wherever possible.

It also helps to make the change "irreversible." In other words program managers need to make sure that there is no reversion back to the old way of doing things. It is also important that organizational designs and performance management systems—recruitment, performance measures, and rewards—are aligned to drive new behaviors.

KATE'S STORY

BACKGROUND

Our company provides professional services to small- and medium-sized organizations.

WHAT HAPPENED

One of the first projects I worked on was the implementation of a document management system. This would, we thought, have massive benefits in filing and sharing documents, saving time and money and paper. A number of the key managers were not so keen. I personally remember spending a lot of time with our finance director to persuade him of the benefits. Eventually he agreed that it was the right thing to do and would not stand in the way of progress.

In fact, when we went live, there was a lot of enthusiasm for the new system. All of the most active users found the system much better. However, after a while we noticed the usage statistics were falling off. There was not as much activity on the system as there used to be.

On further investigation it turned out that the finance director was continuing to use the original paper-based filing system. He was also asking his team to print documents out for him. In turn his team was starting to go back to the paper-based system too, as the finance director was annotating his notes on the paper copies. When I spoke with him again, he said that he would always want a current file in his office. As an interim step, though, we suggested that he archive the older files into the basement as had been our original plan. These files were already scanned into the system. This turned out to be the tipping point.

LESSONS LEARNED

The problem wasn't so much that the finance director didn't want to use the new system. It was more the case that every time he needed to use it, he had to ask someone to show him how. And he had become tired of doing this—hence his reversion to the paper copies. By archiving the old files to the basement, he was now forced to use the system from time to time. And this was enough for him to get used to it. Once he had enough confidence in using it, he used it more and more. Within six months all the files had been moved to the basement. Our lesson learned was basically to make the change irreversible.

2.5 RISK MANAGEMENT: FIVE THINGS TO KNOW

2.5.1 Problems versus risks

Organizations are forever concerned about the future, and effective managers should be looking ahead to see what opportunities exist and also
what potential threats might arise. Nothing is certain about the future,
so how do you decide which risks are worth addressing and which ones
aren't? How do you get to a point where the organization does something about them beyond just fretting?

It is important to have a common way to assess the relative importance of risks. The important questions that we need to ask are:

1. What could go wrong (in general)?

2. What could go wrong (in particular)?

3. What can we do to reduce the chances of that happening?

4. And since we can't be certain of stopping every unfortunate out-
    come, what can we do to minimize the impact were it to go wrong?

So traditional risk management looks at four aspects:

1. What are the general areas of vulnerability?

2. What are the specific potential problems?

3. What are the likely causes of these potential problems and what
    actions can we take to reduce the probability of them occurring?

4. What actions can we take to mitigate the impact if our preventive
    actions fail?

2.5.2 The risk register

An obvious outcome of having a common process for looking at risks is that a number of risks arise from a number of different potential problems. This list of risks is known as the risk register. Having it in one place allows the management team to assess the most important project risks and to agree collectively what is going to be done about them. The risk register typically has the following columns:

1. The general area of vulnerability (this can be the project as a whole, with each project having its own subregister)

2. The owner of the risk. Often there is an incorrect assumption that the project or program manager is the risk owner for all risks. Risks should be "owned" at a level where there is sufficient authority to manage the risk, meaning that some risks can be delegated and some need to be escalated.

3. The probability of this risk happening—this can be given as high, medium, or low or alternatively a score out of 10, where a risk of certain probability is 10

4. The impact on the project if this risk came to pass—again, this can be given as high, medium, or low or alternatively a score out of 10, where a score of 10 means it has a critical impact

5. Actions to reduce the probability of the risk happening and mitigate the impact of the risk happening (shown in column 8, Risk Management)

An example of a typical risk register is shown below[18]:

---

18   Courtesy SofTools Ltd

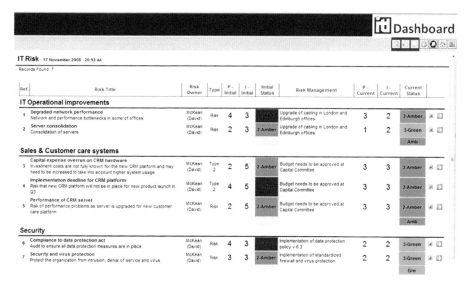

FIGURE 18

If you are overseeing a number of projects, beware of project managers using the risk register to avoid responsibility. Their risk register is closer to a list of everything that might go wrong on the project, including things they are responsible for. The inference is that if they highlight them and the risk turns to reality, they are absolved from responsibility. Clearly this is not the case!

Good project managers recognize that it is impossible to address all risks and to have 100 percent confidence that everything will go according to plan. Their risk registers contain only the most serious risks to the project, with focus on say the top five or ten. When these risks are managed, they fall out of the top ten. New, more serious risks then take their place.

This technique works well for small and simple projects, but traditional techniques quickly get out of their depth when the projects get larger and more complex. A more sophisticated method is needed.

2.5.3 Assumption-based risk analysis

It is a fact that many large, complex projects and programs fail to meet their planned objectives—either failing to deliver what was promised,

sliding the time frames, or exceeding the budget—or all three! Most organizations are undertaking one or more aggressive, "must do" programs at any point in time. These may fundamentally change the way the company conducts its business, and failure to meet objectives on time may have a catastrophic impact on business.

Many different risk management processes are used to improve delivery performance. These may range from very informal approaches, where the lack of process means that it ultimately has little impact, to formal documented processes, which deliver varying degrees of benefit. Very often these "traditional" risk management approaches are sound in theory but disappointing in practice. Some of the reasons include the following:

- A tendency to focus on today's issues rather than tomorrow's risks

- The creation of generic risk statements that are too general to be useful

- An overanalysis using unsubstantiated numerical data

- An underanalysis using misleading high/medium/low-type scales

- Inappropriate prioritization so you "can't see the forest for the trees"

- Inability to get anyone to actually do anything about the risks!

Assumption-Based Communication Dynamics (ABCD)[19] is a highly effective risk management process that captures the collective knowledge and viewpoints from stakeholders on the project. It turns traditional risk management on its head by focusing on what is assumed to be working

---

19   A fuller description of assumption-based risk management, QBC, and Monte Carlo analysis is given in *Risk Management Fast Track to Success*, by Keith Baxter.

rather than what might go wrong. From the list of assumptions that a project is relying on, the focus can then be on why these assumptions might not hold true. The confidence level that an assumption is true is, of course, exactly the opposite of a risk. This is a really important point and is best illustrated with an example. Supposing we think the risk of some key equipment not being delivered on time is 20 percent. Rather than take the glass-half-empty approach, we could take the glass-half-full approach. In other words we could state that we are 80 percent confident that the equipment will arrive on time. Or to put it a different way, we believe that the assumption that the equipment will be delivered on time is 80 percent true.

At the most basic level, ABCD works because it is an intuitive process that takes a positive view of the project (i.e., what assumptions you are relying on to achieve your objectives) rather than a negative one (i.e., what you are expecting to go wrong—your risks). By dramatically improving the communication of key assumptions, risks are avoided or managed proactively, and project objectives are delivered on time.

Other benefits of ABCD include the following:

- It naturally forces people to look to the future (i.e., their assumptions) and therefore ensures true risk management

- It captures specific root causes of risks (i.e., the assumptions)

- It uses a positive outlook and encourages project members to suggest more assumptions they are relying on (and hence more risks)

- It uses meaningful analysis that provides true insight and accurate prioritization

- It provides clear prioritization for senior management as only the most important risks are escalated

- It ensures follow-through on actions via simple but effective roles and governance structures

Assumption-based risk management requires some changes in how risks are assessed. We look at the following:

1. the stability of the assumption (equivalent to probability in traditional risk management)

2. the sensitivity of the project to the assumption (equivalent to impact in traditional risk management)

Once we have clear objectives and plans, program and project managers must ultimately control two fundamental factors if they are to successfully deliver their objectives:

1. The assumptions that underpin the business plan must be clearly identified and communicated.

2. The assumptions made by the individuals in the implementation of the program must be made explicit, rated, and communicated.

Therefore the capture, analysis, and communication of assumptions are critical to the success of the project or program, and this forms the basis of the ABCD process. At the core of ABCD is the analysis of the assumptions. This process uses structured techniques to analyze project plans and identify the most sensitive assumptions that are potentially unstable and therefore the source of greatest risk. Assumptions are rated for sensitivity and stability on an ABCD scale, where A is always "good" and D is always "bad." This provides a meaningful assessment of each assumption (i.e., there is no "medium"!) This also guides the mitigation plans by indicating how best to attack the risk (i.e., stabilize the underlying assumption or desensitize the project to the effects of the assumption).

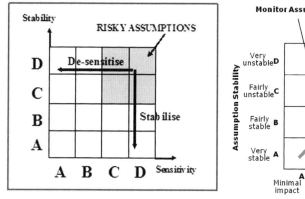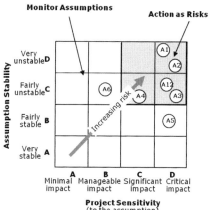

FIGURE 19. ASSUMPTION-BASED RISK MANAGEMENT

2.5.4 A smart way of visualizing risk profiles

The traditional approach of looking at the probability and impact of a risk (or the stability and sensitivity of an assumption) misses one additional dimension—that of urgency. Usually organizations look for the biggest risk and put it top of the priority list. Supposing, though, that the biggest risk on the list was expected to take twelve months to mitigate. Focusing on this might mean that a more urgent or pressing risk is ignored because it is not at the top of the risk register. This problem is often compounded because typically when a project starts, little consideration has been given to the correct sequencing of risk management activities and the overall risk plan.

A good way to show these three dimensions is the risk bubble diagram shown in figure 20, below. Here each risk is represented by an individual circle or bubble on the chart. The height of the risk "off the ground" represents the impact of the risk if it were to be realized. High is good. The lower-impact risks are shown in green. The higher-impact risks are shown in red and are "nearer to the ground." The way to look at this chart is to recognize that unmanaged projects will have risks that

"cluster" around the origin. Bubble diagrams are particularly useful for showing trends in managing risks. The example below on the left shows a project not under control. Over time the risk profile should move toward the situation on the right, i.e., a project that is being properly managed.

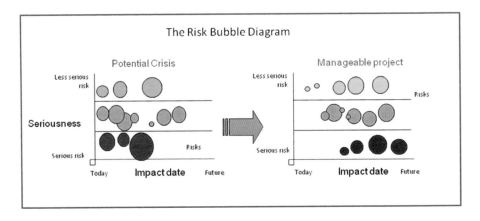

FIGURE 20. RISK BUBBLE DIAGRAM

The second aspect of the risk that this diagram shows is how well it is under control (this is represented by the diameter of the bubble). In other words do we have plans in place to control it? So a risk is controllable if risk plans are in place and there is confidence that they will deliver the intended risk mitigation. A risk is not controllable if there is no plan in place or even if there is that the plan will not significantly reduce it. The larger the diameter of the risk bubble, the less it is being managed.

And so on to the third aspect, the urgency. The x-axis shows the time-line of the project, where the origin of the graph represents the critical objective of the project being met. The x-axis represents how much time is in hand to manage the risk. So the less urgent the risk, the farther away the risk bubble.

So, referring to figure 20 above, the left-hand diagram shows a lot of large red risks close to the origin of the chart, which means that there is

an imminent high probability of severe impact risks with no plan to manage them. The right-hand diagram illustrates a more manageable project. While there are some red risks, these are some way off in the future, and there is a chance to make them more manageable.

In terms of explaining the chart to senior managers, you want as few risks (i.e., bubbles) as possible, those that you have as high off the ground as possible (i.e., lowest impact), as far away to the right as possible (i.e., not yet urgent), and properly managed (i.e., with a small diameter).

2.5.5 Quality-based costing and Monte Carlo

In practical terms the most important question for a risk manager is, "What does the overall risk profile look like, and which are the risks I should manage to make the biggest difference?"

The best technique for solving this problem in the world of projects is called Quality Based Costing (QBC).[20] It quantifies the overall risk profile of a project and then lets you evaluate what impact the mitigation of a particular risk might be on the project. From this you can then work out which are the most important risks to work on.

It will then tell you the following:

• What is the fastest time in which the project can complete?

• What is the most likely time it will take?

• What is the lowest possible cost of the project?

• And what is the most likely cost of the project?

---

20   Theory and examples of ABCD and QBC courtesy of De-Risk Ltd, www.de-risk.com. ABCD risk management is a trademark of De-Risk Ltd.

QBC accurately estimates this for any project. It works by acknowledging the inevitable quality variations in the project (time and cost) estimates and underpins all estimates with their underlying assumptions.

QBC uses the concept of strategic cost "bricks" in the project. Strategic cost means the cost in terms of lost benefits, time, or money spent. The term *brick* is simply used to avoid confusion with work packages, activities, tasks, etc. The size of a brick can vary considerably depending on the stage of project. The first step is to build the "brick wall," and when this is complete, all the bricks together represent the total strategic cost structure of the project (with no estimates at this stage).

Brick owners are allocated for each brick based on the ability to estimate the specific brick as accurately as possible. Brick owners are then interviewed to break down the Brick estimates into their components.

This is done by asking structured questions that break the brick down into:

A =	Absolute minimum
A+B =	Best guess/realistic estimate
A+B+C =	Contingency added
A+B+C+D =	Disaster scenario

The assumptions that underpin the estimates are also captured using the ABCD Assumption Analysis process. The ratings of the assumptions must be consistent with the estimate breakdown. Discussion of these estimates often results in changes to the estimates and/or assumptions to make them more accurate.

Each brick then has two probability distributions built around the estimates: one for the contingency scenario and one for the disaster scenario.

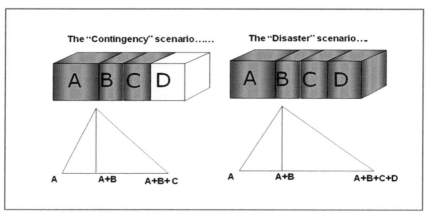

FIGURE 21. ABCD RISK "BRICKS"

Monte Carlo simulations are then run to statistically add the brick esti-mates together. A Monte Carlo simulation is basically where the different possible scenarios are run through the computer using the probabilities set up in the ABCD assessment.[21] The resulting probability distributions can be interpreted to make crucial decisions related to budgeting, pricing, or milestones. The following are some examples:

- There is a "zero" probability of the project costing less than the "base cost"

- The 50 percent confidence cost means that there is a 50-50 chance of the project costing less or more than this value

- The 90 percent confidence cost is normally considered to be the "ideal" cost to budget (if this is considered affordable!)

  The add-up cost is simply the value that would have been reached through "traditional" estimating. The add-up cost could appear any-where on the graph but normally appears below the 50 percent point—it is therefore not surprising that traditional estimating is so far out!

---

21   The calculations shown are illustrations from AssureTM, a web-based tool from De-Risk, capturing ABCD data and generating reports (e.g., risk registers and "bubble diagrams").

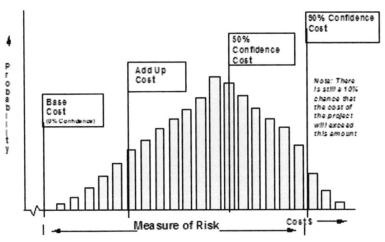

FIGURE 22. MONTE CARLO ANALYSIS

2.5.5.1 Using QBC for competitive advantage

QBC is sometimes used at the proposal stage of a project to provide the best possible information for competitive pricing and to give confidence that crucial milestones will be met. In noncompetitive environments it provides a scientific way of guaranteeing fair budgets and profit. In competitive situations it allows suppliers to understand the level of risk that they are taking on and, if they choose, to cut their price or time scales. It also allows for innovative pricing scenarios that can produce the most aggressive (fixed) price but with reduced risk to the supplier.

Taking it one step further, it can help to bridge a discussion about risk between vendors and their customers. Vendors, for example, have traditionally been very wary of talking about risk. It makes their customers feel that things are expected to go wrong. However, with this kind of Monte Carlo analysis, you can do "what if" calculations to identify which tasks are the most valuable. Vendors can then state which tasks the client should take responsibility for and can clearly demonstrate the positive effect it will have on the project. This also avoids the vendor taking on risks they can do nothing about and those difficult discussions that often ensue.

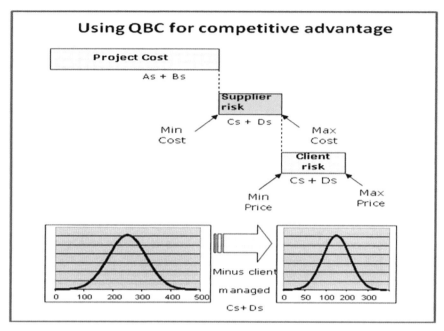

FIGURE 23. QBC FOR COMPETITIVE ADVANTAGE

This analysis can also indicate which areas of risk management to focus on. What you find in practice is that mitigating some activities to ensure that they are guaranteed to deliver earlier makes absolutely little or no difference in the "cost" profile of the project. And small changes to others, or a simple project resequencing, makes a big difference.

2.6 CHANGE LEADERSHIP

2.6.1 IT Managers as the sideline coach

Business change projects with IT at their heart have been around for many years. So, assuming that experiences are shared and lessons learned, why do so many of them go wrong? From all our work with CIOs, at least two things seem clear. First, all change programs depend on people, and emotions can run high. Second, there are program management considerations to take into account, and not all of them will be known at the beginning. Extensive program management experience is needed to take on the changes and still keep the project on track.

Most business change in an organization concerns new products, services, and ways of doing business (processes). The IT department can therefore expect to be at the heart of change in any organization—helping to change the systems that support product design, manufacture, pricing, and sales and marketing, as well as all other internal processes.

Senior IT managers are often involved in major change initiatives. However, they are rarely the primary business sponsor. This sometimes seems unfair as they often have immense experience in delivering major programs. But here is the catch. As soon as a senior IT manager starts taking over a change initiative, it can stop being seen as a business change program and become an IT project. The reality is that IT managers have an extremely difficult task to perform in business change. There are two primary tasks:

1. To monitor progress in the background and apply their business program experience to ensure the success of the change project

2. To coach and guide the business to lead their own change

The role of IT executives is in some ways more difficult than that of the change leader. Using experience from previous initiatives, the IT executive's role is to coach and advise the business change leader of the key areas to focus on to make the business change program successful.

2.6.2 Success guidelines for business change

When it comes to lessons learned, the good news is that there are many. In the table below, you will find our top guidelines, put together from several hundred IT managers who have attended our courses.

Table 8, below, captures these lessons learned using a model of four change phases, namely:

Phase 1: Making the case for change
Phase 2: Starting out
Phase 3: On the change journey
Phase 4: Completing the change program

Phase 1 - Making the case for change

- Look for opportunities for change
- Make sure the organization is ready to take on the challenge
- Be clear on what needs to be delivered for the benefits to be realized. Understand which components / products lead to which benefits so that there is a clear 'line of sight.'
- And make sure the business case really stacks up – just because the numbers are large and positive doesn't make them right. You should always get to the heart of the business case and understand what needs to be delivered for the benefits to be realized

Phase 2 Starting out on the change journey

- Link the vision to the benefits
- Prepare some of the detail ahead of time, for example, enterprise and systems architecture
- Work through the plan and let the users complete the detail so they feel empowered
- Help the business communicate the vision, but remember, this is their job

Phase 3 - On the change journey

- Make sure you are ready to endure the difficult times
- Keep an eye on the benefits through the delivery journey
- Keep programme managing
- Keep the stakeholders engaged
- Keep communicating
- Keep delivering quick wins
- Keep celebrating success

Phase 4 - As the programme nears its end

- Don't give up
- Make sure you prepare for operational mode
- Solve operational problems quickly
- Realize the benefits – measure and review them

TABLE 8. BUSINESS CHANGE SUCCESS GUIDELINES

It also makes sense to have a view of the key lessons learned from the business point of view. There is no better reference than those of John Kotter, professor of leadership at Harvard Business School (so he ought to know!) in his two books, *Leading Change*[22] and *The Heart of Change*.[23] Both books are excellent, but the second is particularly good, with some brilliant case stories illustrating change leadership. Many of his change leadership lessons are included in our list in the previous table.

Leadership and vision are vital ingredients in successful change projects—both from the program team and the senior executives in the organization. It needs to be consistent. It is not acceptable for senior management to join the kickoff meeting with promises of commitment and statements about how important the project is, only for them to be never heard from again. Managers need to be constant supporters of change, and they need to be accountable for its success. Organizations that have a good track record of executive support for change in the past have been shown to consistently have success in the future.

The key lesson in phase two, helping the business communicate the vision, needs a particular mention. A proper shared vision is a vital part of a change project. General high-level statements of intent can often appear nebulous and valueless. In the context of business, vision is about describing what the end will look like. It can be described in any way that works. It can be a rousing statement of future achievement, a video, an animation, or anything that appeals to the mood of the moment. Employees need to have a clear understanding of the vision—it needs to be consistent with the company's strategy, which in turn needs to be consistent with the day to day activities.

2.6.3 The emotional side of (business) change (DREC)

Now for something completely different: brain science. You may have seen some of the images of the brain where scientists trace the energy

---

22   *Leading Change*, John Kotter, Harvard Business Press

23   *The Heart of Change*, John Kotter, Harvard Business Press

coursing through it. Experiments have been done on patients put in unfamiliar situations. In these situations these energy traces show that the prefrontal cortex at the front of the brain lights up. The prefrontal cortex is equivalent to brain RAM. The prefrontal cortex is agile but can only deal with a handful of concepts at one time. When it bumps against its limits, it generates a palpable sense of discomfort, leading to fatigue and sometimes anger. In fact the prefrontal cortex is linked to our primitive emotional center.

Given the choice our brains prefer to use the lower-energy basal ganglia (brain hard drive), which controls habit-based behavior. What the science seems to show is that the brain has a reward mechanism when we gain insights into doing new things—in other words, transferring the workload from one of fear in the prefrontal cortex to one of mastery in the basal ganglia.

So why is this important in business change leadership? Well, it supports the theory that business change can be an emotional journey, causing extremes of behavior in those who are affected. It also suggests, given the reward mechanism for insights, that those who are affected by the change need to be empowered to work through the implications of new change. The role of the change leader is to provide the framework so that the users can master their own destiny, coming to terms with new change.

There is a model that you may have seen before called the DREC curve. It explains the different phases of emotion that people go through when confronting major change. The acronym stands for:

1. Denial

2. Resistance

3. Exploration

4. Commitment

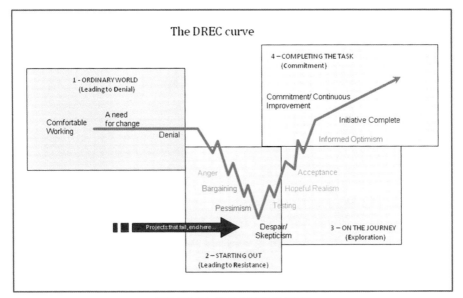

FIGURE 24. THE DREC CURVE

Phase one is our "ordinary world," in other words, the world we live in today. Suddenly a new change program is approved, and the journey begins. If those who are directly affected by the change are not ready or prepared, a number of emotions will come to the surface. The first of these emotions is denial. Users tell themselves, "I can't believe they will really do this." Then as things progress, denial may turn to anger. "This is absolutely the wrong thing for us to be doing. It could severely damage our business."

Emotions may build as the project moves on, often with a bargaining phase. "Why don't we start with the other region first?" Finally they may move on to pessimism and despair, saying, "I don't see how this will ever work."

We come to the bottom of the curve. If the project is going to fail, chances are it will fail here. If we can get past this stage and move to phase 3, then we have a chance of being successful. The project starts to deliver some early results, and those affected may get involved with verifying them (remember what we said previously about delivering step by step). Users may even recognize some value in what is being done. This cautious optimism builds through hopeful realism and even acceptance.

As the project nears completion, there is an informed optimism. Those who have been involved through the change journey are now emerging on the other side. The theory of brain science says they will feel a sense of great satisfaction and achievement.

To summarize, 1) changing the way we do things will often bring about an emotional reaction, 2) large business change may bring about large emotional reactions, and 3) as change leaders we need to recognize the emotional journey and help others to work through it

When you embark on a new change program, think about how it would play out as a script. What would be the denials and the resistance to the program? What sorts of obstacles would you need to overcome? What would the new ordinary world look like? Thinking through a change journey as a film narrative can often be a good way to identify and hopefully address change issues early.

2.6.4 The importance of a good team

Given what we have said in the previous section about the emotional effects of business change, working on business change programs isn't for everyone. And as an IT leader, it is your job to assign the right people to the right change programs. There will often be difficult times to endure, and it is all the more important, therefore, to have a good group of people around you who can work well in such situations. So how do you go about finding these people? The model shown in the matrix below may help you:

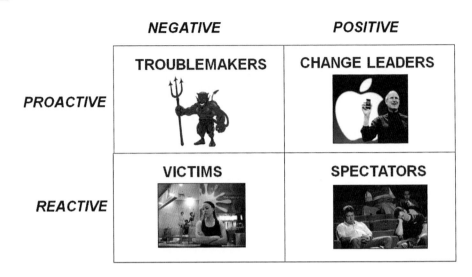

FIGURE 25. ACTORS IN THE CHANGE PROGRAM

This model is a classic Boston matrix, a two-by-two matrix, with positivity of outlook on the x-axis and level of proactivity on the y-axis. So, on the one hand, you need to consider whether someone has a positive or a negative outlook. And second, you will have those who are proactive and those who are reactive. You can see from the Boston matrix above that we end up with four personality types.

JANE'S STORY

BACKGROUND

We obtained approval for a large company-wide change program. I had only been in my post for a short time and had been spending a disproportionate amount of my time looking at the budget numbers. The company had grown quickly through acquisition, and our region comprised five different companies that had been acquired at different times over the previous few years. Two of them occupied the building where my office was situated—an office that was in great need of refurbishment.

WHAT HAPPENED

One of my first tasks was to set the program budget. The finance organization had assigned someone from their department to work with me full-time. The first time that I had occasion to speak to her, I asked if we could meet up. Her office was forty yards down the corridor through some double doors. Unfortunately my security pass would not let me through these double doors. I looked through the small window in the door to the other side. The offices there were very smart, with a plush blue carpet throughout, emphasizing the stark contrast to my side.

I called the finance manager to tell her I couldn't get through. She said that the doors were permanently locked. It was a hangover from when the companies first merged. To get to her office I had to leave my side of the building, walk around to the other reception, sign in, and then be escorted to her office. It seemed everyone had just gotten used to this. But from my point of view, it represented a great fracture in the company and an obstacle preventing everyone from working effectively together. With the agreement of the managing director, we managed to get the doors opened. It became much easier for me to meet with my finance representative, taking care to wipe my feet first.

LESSONS LEARNED

This incident gave me a real insight into some of the rifts that existed in the company. If our change project was to be successful, we needed team members not only from all departments but also from different acquired companies and all levels of seniority. So that is what we did, and the change team performed miracles.

Change leaders (high-energy and positive): Clearly the people you will want on your team are those with a positive outlook and who are proactive—in other words, fast-moving. Surely these are the people you recruited yourself! These are your champions, your change leaders, those you can rely on to inspire others and to make things happen. But as you look around you, you may find that not everyone fits into this category. Keep them informed of everything that is going on. Canvass their input, and adjust your plans accordingly. Seek to provide them with more responsibility, not forgetting to transfer the authority needed to carry it out.

Spectators (low-energy and positive): these are your followers. They will do whatever the program leaders ask of them. Keep them motivated and engaged in the program. Give them opportunities to take on new tasks. Spectators have a positive outlook but typically do not have the same level of inspiration and proactive energy as your proactive change leaders.

Victims (low-energy and negative): Victims often have other things on their minds. They are the ones that can see all the things that could go wrong, but they do absolutely nothing about it. It seems logical to assume that they didn't behave like this when they were interviewed for the job. So presumably something has happened that has caused them to move from positive to negative behavior. Take time to understand their issues. If you are thinking of taking away their responsibilities, speak to them first. Get them to understand why you feel they are not contributing as they should. Keep them informed, even if keeping them motivated is not a good use of your energy.

Troublemakers (high-energy and negative): Troublemakers pose the greatest threat to your project. They are often well connected and can spread rumors and gossip that may undermine what you are setting out to achieve, or they may diminish the value of what you have achieved. What makes things more difficult is that they are usually very clever and fast-moving. And what makes them doubly difficult is that it is not always easy to recognize them. They do not wear a bandana or balaclava.

They will not openly oppose the change, but they will be working in the background, being helpful but in an unhelpful sort of way. If you are the change leader, always be looking out for these people. Spend time with them, and try to turn them around. They are unlikely to be irratio-nal—just obstructive. If possible involve them in part of the project with high kudos. If you can turn them around, it will do untold good to your project.

With reference to Jane's story on the previous page, on her side of the office, people were behaving as victims, and on the finance manager's side, they were behaving as spectators, until Jane took proactive steps to break down the barriers

If the plan for the future is radical, the current team may not possess the skills or desire to make it happen. If so, think about changing the team members. This is easier said than done because you will not only have to recruit the right people, you may also need to move others out of the way. It may have a knock-on effect on the morale of the remaining team members. When making team changes, be bold and make them early.

2.7 OUTLINE OF THE TOP PROJECT FRAMEWORKS

For many years the IT profession was concerned about the high rate of project failure. It seemed that many of the same mistakes were being made again and again. To try to stem the tide of project failure, a number of best practice frameworks were put in place. Two of them, PRINCE2 from the OGC and PMP from the Project Management Institute, are described in the next two sections. Now, let us be clear here. Just because you are using a best practice framework does not mean that your proj-ect will be successful. Many of the reasons for project failure cannot be described in a process manual any more than following a recipe in a cook-book will ensure your cakes will come out perfectly! There will still be projects that fail. Nonetheless, following any methodology is better than not following any methodology. Why? Because a methodology allows you to repeat success rather than to risk failure.

2.7.1 International standards

For any manager to be successful in managing a project, or overseeing a group of projects, clearly he or she needs to have a good method in place.

There have been several attempts to develop project management standards, such as:

PRINCE2: PRojects IN Controlled Environments
Association for Project Management: Body of Knowledge
Capability Maturity Model, from the Software Engineering Institute
The ISO standards ISO 9000, a family of standards for quality management systems
GAPPS, Global Alliance for Project Performance Standards: an open source standard describing competencies for project and program managers

The most common methods are PRINCE2[24] and the PMI[25] method. To find out more, the following two references will help: *PRINCE2 - What You Need to Know* and the *Project Management Book of Knowledge*, and I recommend both for those who are interested in learning more about these methods. In addition, for anyone aspiring to manage or already managing projects, it makes eminent sense to become qualified, and there are many companies worldwide who can provide the accreditations necessary.

2.7.2 PRINCE2

Published by the UK government agency CCTA in 1989, Projects in Controlled Environments (PRINCE) became the UK standard for all government information systems projects. It was upgraded in 1992 to

---

24   *PRINCE2 - What You Need to Know*, © Crown Copyright 2009. Reproduced under license from the Cabinet Office.

25   *Project Management Book of Knowledge* from the Project Management Institute

become the PRINCE2 standard we know today. It is a process-based project management method as opposed to a more adaptive method, such as those found in agile-development-type projects. It has been enhanced over time, with more recent updates in particular making it simpler to use and better integrated with other OGC methods (e.g., ITIL, P3O, P3M3, MSP, and MoR).

PRINCE2 is the framework most commonly used in the United Kingdom. It provides proven best practice and a common vocabulary and can be used on any type of project.

2.7.3 Project Management Institute

The Project Management Institute, Inc. (PMI) standards and guidelines are developed through a voluntary consensus standards development process. PMI administers the process and establishes rules to promote fairness in the development of consensus.

The PMI framework consists of five Project Management Process Groups, each of which is required for every project. The Process Groups have clear dependencies and are typically performed in the same sequence. They are not separate project phases. Projects, particularly IT projects, are of course normally divided into phases or subprojects, such as feasibility study, concept development, design, prototype, build, and test. All of the Process Groups would normally be repeated for each phase.

2.7.4 Agile development

Agile methods are sometimes characterized as being at the opposite end of the spectrum from *plan-driven* or *disciplined* methods such as the PRINCE2 or PMI frameworks.[26] The key theme is that they are versatile, adapting to the speed of changing business requirements, or practically

---

26   In fact, Agile and PRINCE2 are not mutually exclusive. It is possible to use the PRINCE2 governance framework and to treat each SPRINT iteration as a Work Package.

speaking, allowing business users to evolve their ideas through the development process. "We don't know exactly what we want, but we can tell you what we don't want, and we will be able to better explain it if you put something in front of us." Agile methods have much in common with the Rapid Application Development techniques from the 1980s and 1990s.

An adaptive team cannot report exactly what tasks are being done next week—only which features are planned for next month. When asked about a release six months from now, an adaptive team might be able to report only the mission statement for the release or a statement of expected value vs. cost.[27]

2.7.4.1 Agile Manifesto

In February 2001, seventeen software developers published the *Manifesto for Agile Software Development*. Twelve principles underlie the Agile Manifesto:

1. Customer satisfaction by rapid delivery of useful software

2. Welcome changing requirements, even late in development

3. Working software is delivered frequently (weeks rather than months)

4. Working software is the principal measure of progress

5. Sustainable development, able to maintain a constant pace

6. Close, daily cooperation between businesspeople and developers

---

27   We are grateful to VersionOne for their expertise and their summary of agile
       methods which is outlined here. More information can be found on their website
       http://www.versionone.com

7. Face-to-face conversation is the best form of communication (colocation)

8. Projects are built around motivated individuals, who should be trusted

9. Continuous attention to technical excellence and good design

10. Simplicity

11. Self-organizing teams

12. Regular adaptation to changing circumstances

Predictive methods, in contrast, focus on planning the future in detail. A predictive team can report exactly what features and tasks are planned for the entire length of the development process. Predictive teams have difficulty changing direction. The plan is typically optimized for the original destination, and changing direction can require completed work to be started over.

2.7.4.2 Characteristics

There are many specific agile development methods. Most promote development, teamwork, collaboration, and process adaptability throughout the life cycle of the project. The agile method breaks tasks into small increments with minimal planning and do not directly involve long-term planning. Iterations typically last from one to four weeks. Each iteration involves a team working through a full software development cycle, including planning, requirements analysis, design, coding, unit testing, and acceptance testing when a working product is demonstrated to stakeholders. This minimizes overall risk and allows the project to adapt to changes quickly. Multiple iterations are usually required to release a product or new features.

For agile methods to work, stakeholders need to be more closely involved in the development, more tolerant of the software not doing what is required the first time out, but welcoming of the fact that not everything needs to be documented in detail. The teams are often highly collaborative and usually quite egalitarian. It is very helpful for the agile teams to be located in the same office to maximize communication. Although collaborative, the agile team needs a customer representative who is fully committed to the project. One thing we have learned over and over again is that if too many project members are assigned to work part-time on the project, the project will usually fail.

Well-known agile software development methods include the following:

1. Agile Modeling

2. Agile Unified Process (AUP)

3. Dynamic Systems Development Method (DSDM)

4. Essential Unified Process (EssUP)

5. Exia Process (ExP)

6. Extreme Programming (XP)

7. Feature Driven Development (FDD)

8. Open Unified Process (OpenUP)

9. Scrum

10. Crystal Clear

11. Velocity tracking

Some of the main ones are summarized as follows:

2.7.4.3 Scrum

In Scrum, the "product owner" works closely with the team to identify and prioritize system functionality in form of a "product backlog." The product backlog consists of features, bug fixes, nonfunctional require-ments, etc.—whatever needs to be done in order to successfully deliver a working software system. With priorities driven by the product owner, cross-functional teams aim to deliver "potentially shippable increments" of software during successive Sprints, typically lasting 30 days. Once a Sprint's product backlog is committed, no additional functionality can be added to the Sprint except by the team. Once a Sprint has been delivered, the product backlog is analyzed and reprioritized. Scrum has been proven to scale to multiple teams across very large organizations (800+ people).

2.7.4.4 Extreme Programming (XP)

XP promotes high customer involvement, rapid feedback loops, continu-ous testing, continuous planning, and close teamwork to deliver working software at very frequent intervals, typically every one to three weeks. In XP the "customer" works very closely with the development team to define and prioritize granular units of functionality referred to as "user stories." The development team estimates, plans, and delivers the highest priority user stories in the form of working tested software on an iteration by iteration basis. In order to maximize productivity, the practices provide a supportive, lightweight framework to guide a team and ensure high-quality software.

2.7.4.5 Crystal

The Crystal methodology is one of the most lightweight, adaptable approaches to software development. Crystal is actually comprised of a family of methodologies (Crystal Clear, Crystal Yellow, Crystal Orange, etc.) whose unique characteristics are driven by several factors such as

team size, system criticality, and project priorities. Like other agile methodologies, Crystal promotes early, frequent delivery of working software,
high user involvement, adaptability, and the removal of bureaucracy or
distractions. Alistair Cockburn, the originator of Crystal, has released a
book, *Crystal Clear: A Human-Powered Methodology for Small Teams*.

2.7.4.6 Dynamic Systems Development Method (DSDM)

In 1994 the DSDM Consortium was created and convened with the
goal of devising and promoting a common industry framework for rapid
software delivery. Since 1994 the DSDM methodology has evolved and
matured. DSDM specifically calls out "fitness for business purpose" as
the primary criteria for delivery and acceptance of a system, focusing on
the useful 80 percent of the system that can be deployed in 20 percent
of the time.

Requirements are baselined at a high level early in the project. Rework
is built into the process, and all development changes must be revers-
ible. Requirements are planned and delivered in short, fixed-length time
boxes, also referred to as iterations. Requirements for DSDM projects are
prioritized using MoSCoW Rules:

M: Must have requirements
S: Should have if at all possible
C: Could have but not critical
W: Won't have this time, but potentially later

The DSDM project framework is independent but can be implemented in conjunction with other iterative methodologies such as Extreme
Programming and the Rational Unified Process.

2.7.4.7 Lean Software Development

Lean software development is an iterative methodology originally developed by Mary and Tom Poppendieck. Lean software development owes
much of its principles and practices to the Lean enterprise movement

and the practices of companies like Toyota. Lean software development focuses the team on delivering value to the customer and on the efficiency of the "value stream," the mechanisms that deliver that value. The main principles of Lean include the following:

1. Eliminating Waste

2. Amplifying Learning

3. Deciding as Late as Possible

4. Delivering as Fast as Possible

5. Empowering the Team

6. Building in Integrity

7. Seeing the Whole

Lean eliminates waste through such practices as selecting only the truly valuable features for a system, prioritizing those selected, and delivering them in small batches. It emphasizes the speed and efficiency of development workflow and relies on rapid and reliable feedback between programmers and customers. Lean uses the idea of work product being "pulled" via customer request. It focuses decision-making authority and ability on individuals and small teams since research shows this to be faster and more efficient than hierarchical flow of control. It concentrates on concurrent work and the fewest possible intrateam workflow dependencies.

3. Performance Pioneer

3.1 WHAT MORE CAN WE DO?

MOST IT MANAGERS HAVE WORKED IN AN OPERATIONAL ROLE OF ONE FORM OR ANOTHER, EITHER AS A TECHNICAL PRACTITIONER or as team manager. They will have quickly learned that success is dependent on *repeatable processes* of *high quality*.

As far as repeatable processes are concerned, there are a number of frameworks and standards that can act as a guide. By far the most widely adopted is ITIL. The framework itself keeps being amended and updated, but its intent stays the same, namely to provide a reference for best practice in IT service management. Its structure is described in the next section. It is not the only standard, though. By way of completeness, a number of other common standards are described in overview in this chapter. The focus is on how they can enhance performance, even in ITIL-based operations.

So on to the second item: high quality. Different companies define high quality in different ways. It all boils down to having the right metrics and a desire to attain the highest level of performance. Whatever level one seeks to attain, the performance pioneer looks to do it better in the following areas:

- Integrating and aligning IT and business goals

- Demonstrating the value to the business of IT

- Using IT to gain competitive advantage

- Managing constant business and IT change

- Measuring IT organization effectiveness and efficiency

- Demonstrating appropriate IT governance

Before we look at how it is possible to attain more, the following attributes for high-quality IT service management (ITSM) need to be in place to provide a strong foundation:

- People with appropriate skills in the appropriate organizational structure: it is imperative that there are sufficient human resources with appropriate capabilities to do the required work.

- Strong service delivery processes: The design of the processes and the integration between the processes is a key element of ITSM. This must include continual monitoring and improvement.

- Partners of the highest caliber: No organization can work in isolation, so it is imperative that the best are selected to add to the skills of the IT service provider. This can include outsourcing of the main IT operations or something much less.

- Technology that is appropriate for the organization: This may mean the latest state-of-the-art technology and the use of recent developments, such as virtualization and cloud computing, or it may mean something more conservative.

- Technology for effective service management: Appropriate technology that enables delivery of the IT services required by the business, customers, and users must be in place. Any expenditure on technology must be backed by a business case for the need.

So the challenge for IT managers is to work in partnership with the business to deliver high-quality IT services that enable the business as a whole to be successful. The service provider needs a clear view of the business outcomes that are facilitated by the services that are delivered. Too often the IT service provider focuses on the output that they deliver rather than the outcomes that they are facilitating for the business. The focus needs to be on things like "Have more insurance policies been sold as a result of quality IT services?" rather than "Have we delivered more PCs to users?" So when delivering services, it starts with new or changed business requirements and ends with the development of a service solution designed to meet the documented needs of the business.

Service value is measured by the extent to which the service meets customer expectations, and the perceived value should be higher than the cost of obtaining the service. Some value characteristics are as follows:

- Value is defined by customers who will make the final choice, based on a service that represents the best mix of features at the right price.

- Value is not only measured in financial terms.

- Value changes over time and circumstance.

3.2 INFORMATION TECHNOLOGY INFRASTRUCTURE LIBRARY (ITIL)

Adopting best practice will help to close the gap between the capability of the provider and the expectations of the customer. ITIL is the most widely recognized and trusted source of best practice for IT service management applicable to all types of IT service providers. ITIL describes a framework of processes, activities, organization, and roles to form a life cycle approach to IT service management.

A word of caution, though. When implementing ITIL. Sometimes IT managers miss the point and in their enthusiasm to implement, say, an ITIL process framework, take their eye off the day-to-day needs of the users. SLAs are set up that describe how users should log incidents and so on, all fully compliant to a documented process. But when they take a step back, they see that the users are not as well looked after as they were. In other words there is a fine balance to play between structured and repeatable processes and a friendly service that users like.

ITIL was first developed in the late 1980s by the UK government Central Computer and Telecommunications Agency as recognition that IT was becoming an integral part of the operation of every business. Thirty to forty ITIL books were produced in the first version, which did make access somewhat difficult and costly. In the late 1990s and early 2000s, version two was designed and produced by industry experts. In this version the number of books was reduced to eight, and it was then that the global use of ITIL really snowballed. The IP ownership was now with the Office of Government Commerce. In 2007 version 3 was produced (again by industry experts and a very wide global consensus of best practice) with a core set of now five books. In 2011 a version 3 refresh was created with the same architecture. The cabinet office (of the UK government) is now the IP owner of ITIL.

Over the years ITIL has evolved, and its use has grown. It is globally recognized as the best-practice framework. ITIL's universal appeal is that it continues to provide a set of processes and procedures that are efficient, reliable, and adaptable to organizations of all sizes, enabling them to improve their own service provision. Many millions of exams have now been taken on ITIL in over 120 countries. It has been successful because it has the following characteristics:

- Nonproprietary: owned by UK government and not tied to any commercial proprietary practice, solution, or technology platform

- Nonprescriptive: offers robust, mature, and time-tested practices that can be adapted to all types of service organizations (public, private, internal, or external), regardless of size or technical environment

- Best practice: represents the learning experiences and thought leadership of the world's best-in-class service providers

All versions of ITIL have focused on how the IT service provider can align IT services with the needs of the business and customers. The first version was based around disciplines, and the second focused on processes. The third version of ITIL and the current 2011 version moved to a service life cycle approach where the emphasis is on process being just one element of the service provision.

There are five stages in the ITIL life cycle service strategy: Service Design, Service Transition, Service Operation, and Continual Service Improvement. Each of the stages has associated processes within them, and there are many relationships and interfaces between them. The effectiveness of each process depends a great deal on the quality and timeliness of the information exchanged between other processes. There are four key phases.

3.2.1 Service strategy

The purpose of service strategy is to define the perspective, position, plans, and patterns that a service provider needs to be able to execute to meet an organization's business outcomes. It enables the following:

- An understanding of what strategy is

- A clear identification of the definition of services and the customers who use them

- The ability to define how value is created and delivered

- A means to identify service opportunities and how to exploit them

- A clear service provision model that articulates how services will be delivered and funded, to whom they will be delivered, and for what purpose

- Documentation and coordination of how service assets are used to deliver services and how to optimize their performance

- Processes that define the strategy of the organization, which services will achieve the strategy, what level of investment will be required, at what levels of demand, and that ensure a working relationship exists between the customer and service provider

- Activities performed by the service provider to be linked to outcomes that are critical to internal or external customers

- The service provider to have a clear understanding of what types and levels of service will make its customers successful

- The service provider to respond quickly and effectively to changes in the business environment

- Facilitation of communication between the customer and the service provider

- The service provider to organize itself so that it can provide services in an efficient and effective manner

3.2.2 Service design

The purpose of the service design stage of the life cycle is to design IT services, together with the governing IT practices, processes, and policies, to realize the service provider strategy and to facilitate the introduction of these services into the live environment, ensuring quality service delivery, customer satisfaction, and cost-effective service provision.

The objective of service design is to design IT services so effectively that minimal improvement during their life cycle will be required. Embed continual improvement within all service design activities to ensure that the solutions and designs become even more effective over time and to identify changing trends in the business that may offer improvement opportunities. Service design activities can be periodic or exception-based when they may be triggered by a specific business need or event.

There are five elements of service design: design of the technology architecture, the management information systems and tools, the processes, the measurement methods, and the actual service solution for new or changed services.

3.2.3 Service transition

The purpose of the service transition stage of the service life cycle is to ensure that new, modified, or retired services meet the expectations of the business as documented in the service strategy and service design stages of the life cycle. Transition is responsible for managing the actual change, testing the solution, and deploying it to the live environment, which includes early life support.

The objectives of service transition are as follows:

- Plan and manage service changes efficiently and effectively

- Manage risks related to new, changed, or retired services

- Successfully deploy service releases into supported environments

3.2.4 Service operation

The purpose of the service operation stage of the life cycle is to coordinate and carry out the activities and processes required to deliver and manage services at agreed levels to business users and customers. Service operation is also responsible for the ongoing management of the technology that is used to deliver and support services.

Service operation is a critical stage of the ITSM lifecycle. Well-planned and well-implemented processes will be to no avail if the day-to-day operation of those processes is not properly conducted, controlled, and managed. Nor will service improvements be possible if day-to-day activities to monitor performance, assess metrics, and gather data are not systematically conducted during service operation.

As services may be provided, in whole or in part, by one or more partner/supplier organizations, extend the service operation view of end-to-end service to encompass external aspects of service provision—and where necessary shared or interfacing processes and tools are needed to manage cross-organizational workflows.

3.3 SIX SIGMA AND LEAN IT

At the beginning of this chapter, I suggested that performance pioneers who have implemented ITIL processes could look to other standards to give insights as to how they might improve their IT operational and indeed other areas. In my experience some of the techniques of Six Sigma and Lean IT offer the greatest opportunity. Other combinations are no doubt possible too. Six Sigma organizations may look to some of the Lean IT principles to enhance their operational performance. Let us look at both in overview.

3.3.1 Six Sigma

Six Sigma is a business management strategy with a focus on the development and delivery of products and services. It was originally developed by Motorola in the USA in 1986. Today it is widely used in many sectors of industry. Six Sigma seeks to improve the quality of process outputs by identifying and removing the causes of defects (errors) and minimizing variability in manufacturing and business processes. Each Six Sigma project carried out within an organization follows a defined sequence of steps and has quantified targets.

Six Sigma has two key methodologies: DMAIC and DMADV, both inspired by "Deming's Cycle." The W. Edwards Deming Cycle is a repetitive process to determine the next action; it describes a simple method to test information before making a major decision. The four steps in the Deming Cycle are Plan—Do—Check—Act (PDCA). The cycle can be used in various ways, such as running an experiment: PLAN (design) the experiment; DO the experiment by performing the steps; CHECK the results by testing information; and ACT on the decisions based on those results.

- DMAIC is used to improve an existing business process: Define—Measure—Analyze—Improve—Control

- DMADV is used to create new product or process designs for predictable, defect-free performance: Define—Measure—Analyze—Design—Verify

- Focus on developing and delivery of products and services

Six Sigma uses standard deviation to measure the variation of values from the mean. Values are plotted on a distribution chart (histogram) and with enough values will form a bell curve. In a normal (random) distribution, 68.2 percent of values will lie within one standard deviation, 95.5 percent within 2σ, and 99.7 percent within 3σ. A Six Sigma process is one in which 99.99966 percent of the products manufactured are statistically expected to be free of defects (3.4 defects per million).

Key principles from 6σ are:

1. Measure smart

  - Select critical to quality (CTQ) characteristics in the product or process (Y)

  - Each CTQ characteristic is made up of a number of other key variables (Xs) i.e., $Y = f(X)$

- Define performance standards for each characteristic

- Validate the measuring system for each one

- Establish the process capability for achieving them

2. Understand the process

- Define improvement objectives in each Y characteristic

- Identify a few vital initial Xs as sources of variation in Y

3. Test solutions

- Discover the variable relationship among these initial Xs

- Validate the measuring systems

- Establish operating tolerances for these Xs

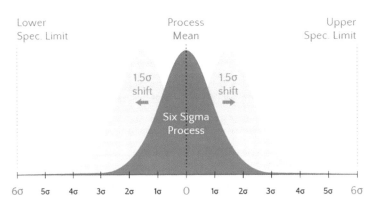

FIGURE 26. ACTORS IN THE CHANGE PROGRAM

Control limits should also be marked for any process. The LCL and UCL show the min and max limits inherent in the process. What you are looking for with Six Sigma is a process where all inputs fall within the upper and lower specification limits, even if the process averages shift 1.5 σ.

3.3.2 Lean IT

When Japanese companies came to fore in the 1980s for their commit-ment to quality, the Japanese words *Kai Zen* (literally meaning "change for the better" but figuratively meaning "continual improvement") first came into common English business usage. This refers to philosophy or practices that focus upon the continuous improvement of processes in manufacturing, engineering, and business management. As part of this, Kaizen involves all employees from the CEO to the assembly line workers and relates to a daily process that humanizes the workplace, eliminates overly hard work, and teaches people how to spot and eliminate waste in business processes.

The Toyota Production System is known for Kaizen and again embeds its philosophy for continual improvement. The Toyota Production System includes a number of principles that have been at the heart of Toyota's success. These principles, originally intended for car manufacture, have a lot of relevance for continual improving IT operations. When applied to the world of IT, the TPS is known as Lean IT. The key principles are:

Management

1. Base management decisions on long-term philosophy

2. Use visual control so problems aren't hidden

3. Go and see for yourself

4. Become a learning organization

Productivity

1. Create continuous process flow

2. Use pull systems to avoid overproduction

3. Level out the workload

4. Use only reliable, thoroughly tested technology

   People and Culture

1. Grow leaders who thoroughly understand the work

2. Develop exceptional people and teams

3. Respect your extended network of partners

4. Build a culture of stopping to fix problems

TPS describes different types of waste. The following list is based on the original seven types of waste but modified as relevant to an IT department:

1. Waiting time, particularly unnecessary time that IT waits for the business and the business waits for IT

2. Inventory: having too much stock, which in the IT world loses value quickly

3. Extra processing: relates to cumbersome IT processes, or, more importantly, software that does not efficiently match a business process

4. Unnecessary motion: relates to people moving around the organization so might include support engineers fixing desk side problems that could have been solved remotely

5. Defects: many things that go wrong in IT might be attributed to this category, for example, software bugs, system failures, etc.

6. Overproducing: producing something beyond what the customer asked for or needs (not the same of course!)

7. Not meeting the needs of the users or customers: this was added to the original TPS list but has particular relevance to IT. It may build on number 1 above, in that if the waiting time for new functionality is too long, by the time the project is delivered, the requirements have changed.

3.3.3 Using Six Sigma and Lean IT to improve ITIL

At the beginning of this section, I suggested that performance pioneers who have implemented ITIL processes could look to Six Sigma and Lean IT to give insights as to how they might improve their IT operational and indeed other areas.

This idea is not completely original. A number of companies have recently combined Six Sigma ideas with lean manufacturing to create Lean Six Sigma. The Lean Six Sigma methodology views Lean manufacturing, which addresses process flow and waste issues, and Six Sigma, with its focus on variation and design, as complementary disciplines aimed at promoting "business and operational excellence." Six Sigma has been used in IT operations to identify problem areas and to measure improvement. Lean IT promises to identify and eradicate waste that otherwise contributes to poor customer service, lost business, higher than necessary business costs, and lost employee productivity.

Lean IT is a good complementary approach. It can almost be used as an innovation technique. So using the list of Lean waste, companies have identified problems in the following:

*   Access privilege problems where front line users were always asking for supervisor over-rides on trivial issues

*   Collaborating teams separated by buildings (time and motion study)

- Multiple versions of software causing high application support costs

- A process sensitive keyboard (that always caused a panic if one broke)

- New starter process that meant new joiners had to wait a week for their PC

- Data center racks built ahead of time that became redundant before they could be used

- Unneeded projects where business priorities had changed

- High calls to service desk that needed a password reset application to be implemented

- Changed approval process that was adjusted so that small changes would not get bogged down

- A service desk process that required the to knowledge system to be updated after each call, but prevented staff from handling urgent calls

Once areas of waste are identified and quantified, it is a relatively straightforward process to implement improvements. Lean IT is not just a method of innovation though. It is a culture. Everyone in the IT team needs to be on the lookout for areas of improvement. To put it another way, they need to have self-awareness to realize that there is a better way of doing something.

Six Sigma is unique in that it provides statistical rigor to measuring defects. In the IT world, we tend to just count them. So for example we might have a Key Performance Indicator (KPI) for fixing different kinds of faults. Let's say we typically resolve faults in an average of twenty minutes. The Six Sigma analysis would guide you to investigate which faults were taking the longest, but also the shortest. One client I worked

with last year with had a very fast average resolution time. But on closer investigation, this was being significantly distorted by password resets that they were doing manually and very quickly!

3.4 CONTINUAL SERVICE IMPROVEMENT IN PRACTICE

The purpose of Continual Service Improvment (CSI), is to align IT services with changing business needs by identifying and implementing improvements that support business processes. These improvement activities support the life cycle approach through service strategy, service design, service transition, and service operation. In effect CSI is about looking for ways to improve service effectiveness, process effectiveness, and cost-effectiveness.

CSI utilizes the Deming cycle of Plan-Do-Check-Act as well as other quality initiatives to enable identification and implementation of improvement to service quality.

To identify improvement opportunities, measuring current performance will be an important factor. Consider the following saying about measurements and management:

> "You cannot manage what you cannot control.
> You cannot control what you cannot measure.
> You cannot measure what you cannot define."

If services and ITSM processes are not implemented, managed, and supported using clearly defined goals, objectives, and relevant measurements that lead to actionable improvements, the business will suffer. Depending upon the criticality of a specific IT service to the business, the organization could lose productive hours and experience higher costs, loss of reputation, or, perhaps, even business failure. Ultimately it could also lead to loss of customer business. That is why it is critically important to understand what to measure, why it is being measured, and carefully define the successful outcome. CSI does the following:

- Review, analyze, prioritize, and make recommendations on improvement opportunities in each life cycle stage

- Review and analyze service level achievement results

- Identify and implement specific activities to improve IT service quality and improve the efficiency and effectiveness of enabling ITSM processes

- Improve cost-effectiveness of delivering IT services without sacrificing customer satisfaction

- Ensure applicable quality management methods are used to support continual improvement activities

- Ensure that processes have clearly defined objectives and measurements that lead to actionable improvements

- Understand what to measure, why it is being measured, and carefully define the successful outcome

The following are practical suggestions from IT managers where Continual Service Improvement has delivered value for them:

3.4.1 CSI in Daily Incident Management

The following ideas may help you with improvements in Daily Incident Management:

- Was the incident logged correctly?

  - include a checkbox for second-line resolvers, asking, "Was the necessary information provided by the service desk?"

  - act upon any negative responses

- clarify standards for information required

- develop scripts with the help of second-line staff

- Checkbox: "Could this have been solved at first line?"

  - highlights areas for improvement through better knowledge documentation and education of the service desk staff

- Analysis of telephony statistics may show opportunities for adjusting service desk staff break times to ensure peak demand is satisfied

- Incident reporting provides an opportunity for first and second line to examine performance and look for reasons for breached targets, inconsistent fix times, reopened incidents, etc. Reports should be analyzed to identify improvement opportunities

- Customer satisfaction questions asked as a routine part of call closure verification will highlight problem areas

- "Did this help?" question for Knowledge Base article highlights poorly written items

  - where many items seem to address the same fault, with little guidance, causing the agent to search through several to find the correct one

  - a better description of symptoms would help avoid this

3.4.2 CSI in Transition

The following ideas may help you with improvements in service transition management:

- Was the change record clear in what was being requested?

- – How often was clarification required, slowing down the process and consuming staff time?

- – What improved guidance could be provided to avoid this?

- Did the change/release take the time/resources specified? If not, why not?

- Were there calls to the service desk following the change by users not understanding how to use the new feature/service?

  - – What improvements to communication methods could be carried out?

- Could issues have been avoided with better testing?

- If we were doing this change/release again, what would we do differently?

3.4.3 CSI in Asset and Configuration Management

The following ideas may help you with improvements in asset and configuration management:

- In addition to scheduled audits of configuration information, the accuracy of the CMS can be checked as part of daily activities

- The service desk analyst checks location and configuration (CI) details with the user

- The service desk analyst identifies unreported staff movements. Information is corrected immediately

  - – Routine checking ensures the records are accurate most of the time

- Saves second line time trying to track down the user later

- Visit remote sites for fault resolution or installation, and take advantage of the opportunity to audit the equipment.

- Provide the second-line engineer with a list of the twenty items that should be present at that location

  - Are they are all still there?

  - Has any unauthorized equipment appeared?

  - Ticking off a short list will not add a lot of time to the visit and will save a separate visit later.

  - As with the earlier point, the more this is done routinely, the fewer errors will be found.

3.5 OTHER QUALITY STANDARDS AND FRAMEWORKS

For completeness the rest of this chapter looks at other common standards that you may come across. The intent is to provide an overview so you can investigate in more detail if you feel they are relevant.

Four standards are looked at:

- ISO/IEC 20000 - 2011

- Control Objects for IT (COBIT)

- Capability Maturity Model Integration (CMMI)

- Microsoft Operations Framework (MOF)

3.5.1 ISO/IEC 20000 - 2011

ISO/IEC 20000 is the international standard for IT service management first produced in 2005 [based on BS15000 produced by the British
Standards Institute (BSI)] with a significant update in 2011. The standard
follows a very similar approach to ITIL with most of the ITIL processes
included. It promotes the adoption of an integrated process approach to
effectively deliver managed services to meet the business and customer
requirements. Part one of the standard comprises ten sections:

1. Scope

2. Terms and definitions

3. Planning and implementing service management

4. Requirements for a management system

5. Planning and implementing new or changed services

6. Service delivery processes

7. Relationship processes

8. Control processes

9. Resolution processes

10. Release process

It is a standard that requires an integrated process approach when
the service provider plans, establishes, implements, operates, monitors,
reviews, maintains, and improves a service management system (SMS).
It is a management system standard (like ISO 9001) that can be used to
assess for compliance. Many hundreds of companies in many countries
are now certified in ISO/IEC 20000. Certification lasts for three years, but

surveillance audits will be conducted by the auditors after one and two years to enable continuation of the certificate.

Increasingly it is a requirement for organizations to achieve this standard to enable them to offer ITSM services to other organizations, especially government organizations.

There are five parts of the standard:

- Part 1: The specification that contains all the mandatory requirements an organization has to meet to achieve ISO/IEC 20000 certification

- Part 2: Guidance and recommendations to support the implementation of part 1

- Part 3: Provides guidance on scope definition and applicability. Used in certification schemes and at the early stages of planning the implementation of ISO/IEC 20000

- Part 4: Process reference model. To be used in future when ISO/IEC 15504-8 is published as a supporting process assessment model for assessing maturity of service management processes

- Part 5: example implementation guide

ISO/IEC 20000 is aimed at organizations running an IT service, whether internal or external.

ISO/IEC 9001, the generic quality standard, and ISO 27001, the information security standard, are also widely used in IT operations.

3.5.2 COBIT

Control OBjectives for Information and related Technology (COBIT) is another widely utilized framework in the ITSM area. ISACA (Information

Systems Audit and Control Association) is a membership organization serving IT governance professionals globally and with its affiliate, the IT Governance Institute (ITGI), develops and produces COBIT.

COBIT was first released in 1996. COBIT 5 connects to other frameworks such as ITIL and provides renewed, authoritative governance and management framework for enterprise information and related technology, building on 4.1 and linking and reinforcing all other major ISACA frameworks and guidance, such as the following:

- Board Briefing on IT Governance

- Business model for information security™(BMIS)™

- IT assurance framework™ (ITAF™)

- Risk IT framework

- Taking governance forward

- Val IT™ Framework

COBIT is a framework and a knowledge base for IT processes and their management and not a standard as such—an organization cannot be certified against it, but COBIT does contain metrics that can be measured, and some can be benchmarked in COBIT Online.

The business focus of COBIT links business goals to IT goals, provides metrics and maturity models to measure their achievement, and identifies the associated responsibilities of business and IT process owners. The process focus of COBIT is illustrated by the process model, which subdivides IT into thirty-four processes in line with the traditional IT responsibilities of Plan, Build, Run, and Monitor, providing an end-to-end view of IT. Enterprise architecture concepts help identify the resources essential for process success, i.e., applications, information, infrastructure, and people.

COBIT is an enterprise-wide framework that addresses the governance and management of enterprise information and technology assets to achieve stakeholder business objectives. It defines RACI (Responsible, Accountable, Consulted, and Informed) charts for role allocation and inputs/outputs, and guidance on organizational structures, skills, and competencies. It organizes IT activities into a process model to ensure resources are indentified and coordinated across the organization.

COBIT supports regulatory compliance (for example, the ISACA publication IT control objectives for Sarbanes-Oxley enables organization to prepare for a Sarbanes-Oxley audit) by providing a framework approach that will make it easier to identify and prove compliance to any applicable standard or requirement.

3.5.3 CMMI

Capability Maturity Model Integration (CMMI) is a process improvement approach whose goal is to help organizations measure and improve their performance. CMMI can be used to guide process improvement across a project, a division, or an entire organization. Currently supported is CMMI Version 1.3.

CMMI was developed by a group of industry experts and the Software Engineering Institute (SEI) at Carnegie Mellon University. CMMI models provide guidance for developing or improving processes that meet the business goals of an organization. A CMMI model may also be used as a framework for appraising the process maturity of the organization.

It enables assessment and benchmarking of an organization's IT processes and helps to guide process improvement and set improvement goals, integrate separate functional groups, and provide a point of reference for process appraisal. CMMI can be (and often is) used to measure ITIL/service management processes. CMMI-SVC is for IT services.

There are five levels of maturity within CMMI, and different definitions are sometimes used, but basically they are as follows:

- level 1 initial: process unpredictable

- level 2 repeatable or managed: reactive

- level 3 defined: proactive

- level 4 quantitatively managed: measured and controlled

- level 5 optimizing: process improvement

In ITSM terms these are typically used to measure the various process maturities so that an organization could be level 1 in some areas and level 5 in others.

3.5.4 Microsoft Operations Framework (MOF)

Originally the Microsoft Operations Framework (developed by Microsoft to enable organizations to utilize Microsoft software in a better way within IT operations) was based on ITIL and built on ITIL in some areas. The goal of MOF is to provide guidance to IT organizations to help them create, operate, and support IT services while ensuring that the investment in IT delivers expected business value at an acceptable level of risk.

MOF's purpose is to create an environment where business and IT can work together toward operational maturity, using a proactive model that defines processes and standard procedures to gain efficiency and effectiveness. MOF promotes a logical approach to decision making and communication and to the planning, deployment, and support of IT services.

MOF consists of integrated best practices, principles, and activities that provide comprehensive guidelines for achieving reliability for IT solutions and services. It provides guidance that allows you to determine what is needed for your organization now, as well as activities that will keep the IT organization running efficiently and effectively in the future. MOF also encompasses all of the activities and processes involved in managing an IT service: its conception, development, operation, maintenance,

and retirement. It organizes these activities and processes into Service Management Functions (SMFs).

The current version of MOF, 4.0, describes the IT service life cycle in terms of three phases and a foundational layer:

- The plan phase focuses on ensuring that, from its inception, a requested IT service is reliable, policy compliant, cost-effective, and adaptable to changing business needs.

- The deliver phase concerns the envisioning, planning, building, stabilization, and deployment of requested services.

- The operate phase deals with the efficient operation, monitoring, and support of deployed services in line with agreed-to service level agreement (SLA) targets.

- The manage layer helps users establish an integrated approach to IT service management activities through the use of risk management, change management, and controls. It also provides guidance relating to accountabilities and role types.

3.5.5 Notable Names of Quality

There are several quality frameworks and methods used with IT operations:

Dr. Joseph Juran was one of the first people to consider the cost of poor quality and said that the quality is a management responsibility. He described the quality trilogy as being composed of three managerial processes:

- Quality planning supported by planning methodologies

- Quality control supported by control methodologies

- Quality improvement supported by improvement methodologies

Italian Vilfredo Pareto created a mathematical formula to describe the unequal distribution of wealth in his country, observing that 20 percent of the people owned 80 percent of the wealth. Joseph Juran conceptualized the formula and called it the Pareto 80/20 rule, observing the "vital few and trivial many," the principle that 20 percent of something are always responsible for 80 percent of the results.

The 80/20 rule means that in anything a few (20 percent) are vital and many (80 percent) are trivial. In Juran's initial work he identified 20 percent of the defects causing 80 percent of the problems. Project managers know that 20 percent of the work (the first 10 percent and the last 10 percent) consume 80 percent of your time and resources. You can apply the 80/20 rule to almost anything.

Dr. Kaoru Ishikawa designed quality circles for the following purposes:

- Support the improvement and development of the company

- Respect human relations in the workplace and increase job satisfaction

- Draw out employee potential

He also designed fishbone (or Ishikawa) diagrams, also referred to as a cause-and-effect diagrams. These are used to draw out the factors that might affect a particular quality characteristic, outcome, or problem.

An Ishikawa diagram is typically the result of a brainstorming session in which members of a group offer ideas on how to improve a product, process, or service. The main goal is represented by the trunk of the diagram, and primary factors are represented as branches. Secondary factors are then added as stems, and so on. Creating the diagram stimulates discussion and often leads to increased understanding of a complex problem.

4. Crisis Commander

UNFORTUNATELY, MANY CRISIS SITUATIONS ARE CAUSED BY PROB-LEMS WITH IT. IT COULD BE SOMETHING AS CLEAR-CUT AS A SERVER that has a hardware fault. Or it could also be a malicious attack from outside. The crises that IT needs to handle are wide-ranging and include fires, floods, earthquakes, and so on. Even if the technical systems aren't directly affected, there is still the issue of ensuring that people can still continue to work relatively unaffected.

Business continuity planning (avoiding a crisis in the first place) and crisis leadership (taking command when it does) are vital skills for the IT manager.

In this chapter we discuss four key aspects:

1. Crisis planning

2. Crisis management

3. Problem solving techniques

4. Communications in crisis

4.1 A FRAMEWORK FOR INFORMATION SECURITY

Being thrown into the middle of a crisis can be very unnerving. The typical crisis that IT managers handle relates to failures in technical equipment. Even technical failures can render a company completely helpless, and in some cases the crisis can be even more serious, involving injuries to personnel and worse. All eyes are on the IT department to resolve technical problem quickly and get vital systems back up and working. Even if the failure was in no way the fault of the IT department, for example malicious attacks, a cloud of blame can all too quickly descend. So without a doubt, the best plan is to avoid crises happening in the first place. And to do this in a structured way requires a good framework. And of course the good news is that experts have already created one. The best and most widely used is probably the ISO 27001 standard. It is a comprehensive set of controls comprising best practices in information security.

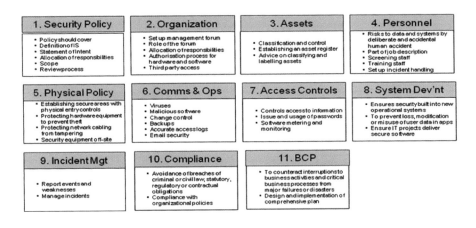

FIGURE 27. THE ISO 27001 STANDARD

In outline it groups security and crisis issues into one of eleven categories:

1. Security policy, covering all the aspects of information security, including definitions and responsibilities

2. Organization, including the governance function and authorization

3. Assets, including their classification and control

4. Personnel security, responsible for assessing and protecting against risks to data and systems by deliberate and accidental human actions

5. Physical security, covering the establishment of secure areas with physical controls and the protection of hardware and other assets from theft

6. Communications and operations, including protecting against viruses and malicious software

7. Access controls, ensuring that the right people have access to the right systems

8. System development, relating to the embedding of security in software development

9. Incident management—the resolution of security issues

10. Compliance, ensuring that there are no breaches of criminal or civil law and that systems comply with regulatory and organizational rules and policies

11. And finally, business continuity planning, or BCP for short, is concerned with keeping the business running, reducing the chances of anything going wrong and its impact on the business.

4.2 CRISIS PLANNING

It is not possible in these pages to provide a detailed description of crisis planning. A good reference is *Security Planning and Disaster Recovery*, by Maiwald and Sieglein.[28] Reading on the subject is helpful. In practice, though, it makes more sense to bring in experts who have experience

---

28 *Security Planning and Disaster Recovery*, Maiwald and Sieglein, ISBN - 0-07-222463-0 published by Osborne.

from many different clients and who can help you put in place a robust and practical plan suited to your own organization.

The crisis commander is particularly concerned with the last of these, namely business continuity planning and making sure that we have good contingency plans. Most companies have crisis plans in place, and if you have just taken on responsibility for this area, that is just as well, as creating all of the following from scratch would be a massive task. Best practice suggests nine steps to prepare to respond should the worst happen:

- Create a good inventory of hardware and software and network connectivity

- Build a table of the critical business systems and outage parameters

- Use scenario planning to create a table of potential disasters and their probability and impact

- Identify and budget recovery options

- Set up the crisis management team (CMT) and assign responsibilities

- Agree and sign off on the disaster response plan

- Prepare disaster recovery environment (including a crisis response center, backup comms equipment, contact lists, backups, etc.)

- And finally, practice response with the crisis response team with realistic simulation

Crisis planning is ongoing. It will *help* prevent crises, and it will *help* you respond better. But it won't *prevent* crises because many crisis situations are the result of changes made since the plans were updated or indeed intentional acts designed to get around your prevention plans. So, in one example of fraud, an employee was taking cash payments from customers on their site, issuing them a receipt, and manipulating the

systems to make the invoice appear paid. It was this manipulation that caused systems crashes from time to time. And this was in a company where plans were updated every six months and employees rigorously vetted. All the security and planning in the world won't help if technically intelligent (but morally stupid) people are involved in overcoming your systems.

On another occasion carefully designed security systems were highly effective in preventing the IT systems from switching over to a backup network when two of the key staff happened to be off sick. So never go into a crisis and expect that all of your preparations will solve everything for you. Systems need to provide you with the information and diagnosis, and if you are lucky, backup systems will take over, but not always. Newspapers provide a constant reminder of how easy it is for leading companies with advanced systems and processes can be thrown into crisis. Recent examples that all occurred in a relatively short time include Apple, Sony, Blackberry and the Royal Bank of Scotland.

Fortunately, though, crisis management teams that undertake regular crisis simulations perform better in real crises. The process of simulating and practicing a crisis situation allows team members to respond better and identify equipment, processes, and actions that can be put in place that will subsequently aid them when a real crisis hits.

4.3 WHEN DISASTER STRIKES

Let us assume that despite our best planning efforts, a crisis of some sort has struck. By its very nature, it is unlikely that you will know in advance. There are some situations where there is advance warning, for example, hurricanes in the Caribbean or tornadoes in the USA. In Indonesia we also got a limited advanced warning of an earthquake. Because of the immense distances and the fact that earthquakes travel at around 3 km/sec, we had a warning of about fifteen minutes. Generally crises are less accommodating though. The first warning may come from someone on the IT operations bridge, a phone call from a customer, or even the television news.

Crises can take one of many forms:

- Fire in an office building or the data center

- Severe weather conditions, such as high winds, snow, and rain (flooding)

- Grid power outages

- Cyber attacks

- Physical attacks

- Extortion

- Civil unrest

- and so on…

Experienced managers repeatedly tell us that high-quality crisis planning and systems resilience (i.e., having working backup systems in alternative locations) and a good response team will help more than anything else. In general, whatever the crisis, a team needs to have a crisis response process that has been practiced to guide it through a robust response. The most effective crisis response teams work in three groups:

- A crisis management team in charge of the overall crisis leadership and control

- A problem resolution team, looking to mitigate problems and start recovery

- A communications team for both internal and external communications

For any practical crisis response, define the roles and responsibilities clearly in advance. The key roles will normally include the following:

- The chairperson who will lead the Crisis Management Team

- A business operations expert who understands all the key operational aspects and risks of the business

- A spokesperson who has experience and the authority to speak to the media if required

- A coordinator

- And co-opted functions, such as legal support, which are brought in when required

4.3.1 Crisis response: First actions

In a real crisis situation, there is barely enough time to think. If a group is not properly organized, they will be constantly interrupted by people wanting to know what is happening and providing updates to the situation. It is important that the Crisis Management Team can focus on what is important. A key part of this is the handling of the phones and other messages coming in. The best way to do this is with a special "filter team." This will be a group of experienced professionals who are able to stay calm and separate critical information coming in from less important information. Often the PAs to the board of directors are highly skilled at this. Whoever they are they need to be trained in crisis response.

As soon as the crisis management team has formed, its role will be to assess the situation, take control and issue commands, and communicate effectively. The chairperson must also be prepared to lead and dictate. This is not a "nice" situation, and tough measures will be called for. Some people are not well suited to this brutal environment and should not be part of the team.

For many IT crises, communication is normally important but under-emphasized. Most communication takes the form of an e-mail sent to users telling them that one of the systems has gone down and they will be kept posted of progress. The users in turn take the responsibility to tell customers and other callers of any disruption. However, for a more serious crisis, the role of the communications team goes beyond this. It is true that the IT function as such will rarely appear on television or radio, but they need to be aware of the importance of the communication and be prepared to provide useful information to the comms team when required.

In some situations it is not possible to convene at the preagreed location, either because it has been damaged or is cordoned off or for some other reason. A backup location needs to have been identified and hopefully also prepared for such an incident. Similarly, in some situations there is a need for a reserve CMT in the case that the main team is away on leave or perhaps injured in the crisis. In one major retail bank, several meeting rooms have signs on the doors stating that they are earmarked for crisis response and meeting participants may be ejected should the room be required.

These meeting rooms had been specially prepared with additional phone lines, televisions connected to different media stations, and so on. The communications management team will generally assemble in a preagreed location such as this. This location needs to be properly prepared, ensuring that there are good communications services as well as a television and radio to monitor the media reporting.

Once the crisis team has assembled, it is important to put actions in place to contain the situation. There are five recognized rules of containment as follows:

1. Set up the CMT and act quickly and decisively. Delay will only allow the incident to grow worse.

2. Put people first: Corporate reputation can be repaired, but the lives of customers and employees cannot.

3. Put the response team to work—an experienced team working together.

4. Be on the crisis scene quickly—this demonstrates that the crisis is being taken seriously.

5. Communicate to all—it's the best way to counter rumors and speculation.

   In looking to identify the scope of the crisis, the following checklist can be used as an aide-mémoire for the key resolution activities:

1. Provide information to emergency responders.

2. Assemble or build the technical response team.

3. Assess damage to the building or buildings and key areas within them.

4. Determine the status of power and water.

5. Determine the status of key systems and communications.

6. Start the problem solving process.

7. Keep the CMT informed.

4.3.2 Crisis response: Resolving the issues

Trying to fix a difficult technical problem when everyone around is in a state of panic is particularly tough. In one company a senior director was particularly disruptive in such situations. Whenever a technical outage occurred, someone was assigned the role of finding him and basically distracting him so he could not interfere. Amusing as this was, it emphasizes the importance of letting the IT specialists get on with the job of resolving the problem. The other problem that is frequently encountered is with

so-called heroes. These are people who love to be the center of attention when things go wrong. They charge off, making ad hoc changes to
systems because they think they know what the problem was. It is not
unusual to find "hero" specialists not just making the situation worse, but
actually causing the problem in the first place.

Sometimes, however, problems occur for a combination of reasons,
and guessing will only make things worse. The film *Apollo 13* is an accurate representation of what really happened on that flight. It gives a fas-
cinating account of real and practical problem solving using a technique
that has been proven to be effective in difficult situations based on the
following process.

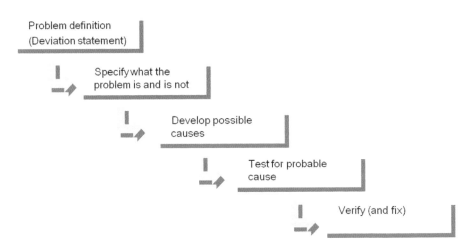

FIGURE 28. THE PROBLEM SOLVING PROCESS

It is important therefore for the technical resolution team to have a
structure in place to resolve key issues. The recommended problem solving process shown in figure 28 follows five basic steps:

1. Define the problem in a clear way.

2. Gather specific information around the problem, defining what the
    problem is and what it isn't—in other words what is working com-
    pared to what isn't.

3. Develop possible causes of the problem.

4. Test for probable cause.

5. Finally, having tested the most probable cause, verify that this is really the problem after all, and fix it.

There is an example where a customer wrote to the chief executive of Pontiac, complaining that whenever he bought vanilla ice cream, his car would not start. To cut a long story short, it turned out that the vanilla ice cream was kept in a separate case at the front of the store, unlike the chocolate or strawberry, for example, which was at the back. What the engineers discovered, therefore, was that the customer returned to his car more quickly when he bought vanilla ice cream. Having understood the possible difference in the situation, the engineers could go about resolving the problem, which (assuming the story is true!) turned out to be a vapor lock that did not dissipate in the shorter time it took to buy vanilla ice cream. Although a slightly odd example, it does illustrate that a robust problem solving process is vital for successful IT crisis management.

4.3.3 Communicating in a crisis

If the crisis is serious enough that it attracts local or national media attention, time is of the essence. In today's fast-moving online world, news can be broadcast within minutes of it happening. The media business talks about the "golden hour," which is the critical period for your crisis response. In this golden hour, keep the following timeline in mind:

Let us assume that the crisis has just happened. The chances are that the crisis management team is just assembling and very little is known about what has actually happened and what caused it.

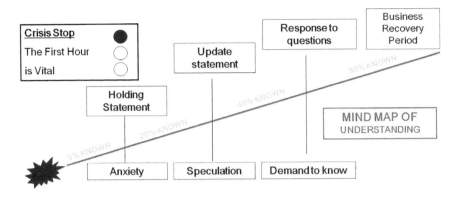

FIGURE 29. THE GOLDEN HOUR

The first thing to worry about is people—particularly those involved in the incident and also their family and friends. Issue a holding statement at the earliest opportunity, typically within twenty minutes. Yes, twenty minutes is all you have if you want to maintain control of the situation. Make the statement short and factual, confirming that there has been an incident, some outline information as to what has happened, and a contact number for concerned family and friends. Keeping people informed is a vital role to keep rumor and speculation to a minimum. Provide updates to your original statements on a regular basis.

Depending on the seriousness of the crisis, it may well be that one of your senior staff needs to respond to questions at a press meeting. At this time it is important that only the facts as they are clearly known are given and that any responses to questions are helpful but carefully chosen.

The final stage in the media cycle is the recovery phase. Here you will learn lessons about what went wrong, and you will want to assure your customers, employees, investors, and other stakeholders that you have put in appropriate measures to prevent a recurrence.

Media training is something that requires practice, and it is unlikely that you, as an IT manager, will be required to do this. Do not ever attempt this unless you have been fully trained in front of cameras with experienced journalists.

To summarize, the following are the essential activities for crisis leadership:

1. Preparation, evaluating risks, and having a contingency plan in place and a signed-off communications policy

2. Practice and gain confidence in a controlled environment, practicing crisis control, problem resolution, and media communications skills under pressure

3. Encourage skills to develop leadership, teamwork, and good communication

5. Commercial Expert

COMMERCIAL SKILLS ARE VITAL TO THE SUCCESS OF ANY IT MANAGER. WE LOOK AT THE FOLLOWING:

1. Setting sourcing strategy

2. Making good sourcing decisions

3. The art of negotiation

4. Finance for IT managers (managing budgets and business case calculations)

5.1 SOURCING STRATEGY

The foundation for good sourcing is a good sourcing strategy, ensuring that the sourcing initiatives you embark on are part of a clear plan with clear objectives.

The sourcing process described here is one that has been developed over a period of time and is a variation of the process described in chapter 2. It takes some of the standard strategy principles and applies them to IT sourcing in particular. Like any good strategy, it starts with the business context and then sets some sourcing objectives. Typical sourcing objectives might include the following:

- Maintain or improve quality of service

- Business process improvements

- Access to skills and best practice

- Cost savings; gain advantages of economies of scale

- Improve versatility, control, and responsiveness

- Improve resilience or supplier dependence (multiple suppliers)

- Reduce supply chain risk

- Technical innovation

- Provide a better career path for (IT) staff

- Consistency with company culture

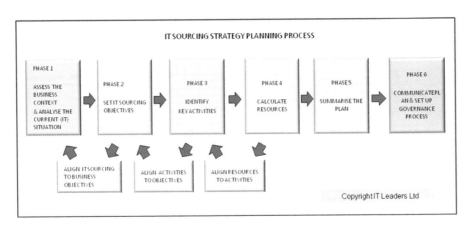

FIGURE 30. THE IT SOURCING STRATEGY PROCESS

As with any strategy development, there are a number of possible initiatives that may come out of the strategic sourcing evaluation to meet

the sourcing objectives. Initiatives tend to fall into one of a number of types:

1. Small and medium contract agreements: typical activities include renewal on the same terms, renewal on better terms, or tendering for alternative suppliers and managing the portfolio in a structured way

2. In-house processes: options include continuing with the existing arrangement, reviewing options for sourcing, or moving straight to an outsource solution

3. Outsourced processes: options include continuing (or renewing) the existing sourcing arrangements, reviewing options to transfer to an alternative sourcing partner, or bringing the solution back in house

One good way to assess whether a process is suitable for sourcing is to look at the quality of the final outcome and how easy it might be to make it happen. Some guidelines are given in the table below:

Quality of final business outcome	Ease of making it happen & maintaining it
Fits with company strategy – so for example, it maintains competitive advantage, complies with company values, ethics and brand (30%)	Business risk – changes in environment (measured with PESTEL), such as company restructures mean that it may be a good idea now, but not in the future (30%)
Improves efficiency – so for example, it delivers the best financial benefit e.g. total cost of ownership (including own partner management), improved service levels and process efficiency (with few business dependencies on you) (30%)	Financial risk (including taxes, reverse taxation, future wage increases, unknown costs etc.) (30%)
Provides additional or hard to find expertise and resources that respond quickly to changing business conditions in a versatile and scalable way (20%)	Partner has the skills & experience needed and you can build a strong positive relationship and be able to manage them (20%)
Conforms to your compliance and security requirements, for example, providing the necessary protection of your data (20%)	The actual transfer project is manageable – the problem is known, knowledge transfer is straight forward, resources from both sides are available and the size of the opportunity is big enough to be worth the management effort (20%)

TABLE 9. GUIDELINES FOR OUTSOURCING

Using this table we can then plot each process using the chart below. Each sourcing process is represented with a dark-blue ellipse, showing how suitable the process is for being sourced and the risk in making it happen.

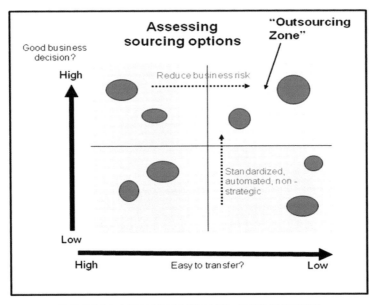

FIGURE 31. RISK FIT MATRIX FOR OUTSOURCING

From the diagram you can see that the opportunities most suitable for sourcing will be those in the top right-hand corner. Often the main reason why a process is not suitable is around the fact that the process is not well managed, standardized, or automated. Sourcing wisdom has it that processes must be under control for a sourcing arrangement to work. It may be that a sourcing partner can help your internal team to put some of this control in place. Similarly, the only way that high-suitability but high-risk processes should be outsourced is when the risks have been properly mitigated. There are many situations when this never happens. In other words there are some processes that should never be outsourced because they are too strategic to the organization.

Of course, sourcing is not just a yes or no decision. There are a number of options that may help to reduce the risk of working with sourcing partners. The following diagram gives an illustration:

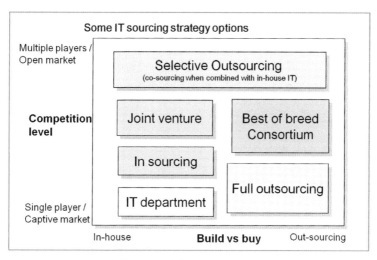

FIGURE 32. IT SOURCING OPTIONS

The options are as follows:

1   Selective outsourcing: many vendors are chosen to provide IT ser-
    vices. When this is done in combination with the internal IT depart-
    ment, this is called co-sourcing

2   Joint venture: a formal legal structure is set up between the organiza-
    tion and an outsource partner. IT staff can often choose whether to stay
    as employees of their company or work for the joint venture partner

3   In-sourcing: the IT department takes over a service that was previ-
    ously outsourced. IT departments put commercial principles around
    the IT services to more closely mirror outsource conditions. The gen-
    eral view is that can be a dangerous route, reducing flexibility and
    causing IT to be viewed as distant.

4   IT department: the IT department provides all the major IT services
    (it may have support agreements with software providers for level
    three support)

5   Full outsourcing: one outsource partner provides all the IT services
    for a host organization

6   Best-of-breed consortium: where the host organization chooses a small number of strategic partner to provide the IT services

5.2 AVOIDING BAD DECISIONS

Any change to your sourcing landscape will inevitably mean going to the market to evaluate and ultimately choose a sourcing solution. But beware! There are many pitfalls in making sourcing decisions. Here are five common examples:

1. Decision blindness (making the wrong decision): Organizations sometimes go down a path thinking that their only option is to select a particular supplier for a particular need. To avoid making mistakes at this level, it makes sense to ask questions around the key decision statement. So what is it we are really trying to decide? Can we broaden our decision and end up with a better outcome? (See Ian's story below.) BBC's *Horizon* program gave a very interesting example where taxi drivers work longer in hot weather when business is harder to come by. This is illogical since they could earn much more money by working slightly longer in bad weather, when everyone is looking for a taxi. The illogicality is caused by a belief that they should earn a fixed minimum amount every day rather than maximize their income.

2. Anchoring on the wrong information: Anchoring is a well-known decision trap. It happens when personnel have in mind that particular outcomes are likely when certain decisions are made. These decisions can often be based on incorrect information, for example, data that is out of date or applied to a previous organization. The term comes from the decision being anchored (or biased) towards the first idea or number suggested (often rules of thumb from previous experience).

3. Trying to handle too many data points at the same time: A common mistake is where supplier evaluations are made on such a large number of items that it is impossible to make a rational comparison.

It is better to group criteria into some high-level components. Our experience tells us that there are probably six main components, namely, the quality of the supplier organization, the functionality of the solution, the quality of the technical solution, the quality of implementation, the support services, and the total cost of ownership. Aggregating all the requirements into these six categories means that a useful decision is easier to make.

4. Assuming that a group of clever people will automatically make the right decision: This is a common fault where everyone in the room assumes that the others in the room have experience in the particular area. It is helpful to have an opinion from an outside expert.

5. Making the decision too early: Many organizations feel they have to move as fast as possible on everything. Sometimes delaying a decision can help in many ways, particularly if the organization is busy on other initiatives. In IT delaying procurement typically means that better solutions at lower prices become available.

6. Buying more than is needed: salespeople are incentivized to encourage you to buy more earlier. When we review common sourcing mistakes, this comes up very frequently. You should only buy software licenses for users you know will be using the software.

IAN'S STORY

BACKGROUND

One of our smaller operational units was about to launch a series of new products. The customer order system that was being used was not well liked by the users and had become progressively more difficult to use. The business saw this as an opportunity to buy a top-end replacement. The new system provided lots of functionality and was highly configurable.

WHAT HAPPENED

The new system took nine months to implement instead of the predicted six months. It turned out to be very sophisticated (i.e., complicated) to use, and it was also very difficult and expensive to support. After a year a new general manager was appointed. When he saw the support costs, he scrapped the system immediately and directed the operation to upgrade the previous system.

LESSONS LEARNED

It was a classic case of decision blindness. The users had become so frustrated with the old system but had not realized that with some reasonable investment, all of the old problems were fixable. They had become so focused on buying a new system that they never stopped to think if they were asking the right question. The question they asked was, "How can we replace the existing system with a fancy new one?" The correct question was, "What is the best way to overcome the serious usability problems we have with the functionality to launch the new products?"

5.3 THE ART OF NEGOTIATION

Negotiation is a key skill at the heart of business. While few of us would consider ourselves professional negotiators, as an organization we are frequently surprised by how few technology managers have had any formal negotiation training. Our view is that there is easily a 10 percent variance "up for grabs" in any negotiation that will go to the better negotiator. Remember, negotiation isn't just about money either. It can be about quality of support, flexibility, and performance too.

When you consider that most IT managers are negotiating tens of thousands if not millions of dollars, euros and other currencies every day, the benefits of doing it well and consequences of doing it badly are huge. So going back to basics, negotiation is a process of give and take where the conditions of a transaction are agreed and acted upon. Negotiation is all about movement, in essence moving from the initial views of the two parties to a central position where a common agreement is reached. The principle of movement is very important, and the best negotiators not only understand this but also use differing approaches to get to a desired result.

Finally, logical reasoning is a very powerful tool and one that top negotiators use to good effect. We all like to consider ourselves reasonable people and will therefore feel some obligation to consider any reasoned argument. In our negotiation role plays, we see considerable differences in the outcomes of those parties that use logical arguments versus those that don't.

Research has shown that there are two key but separate skills that are needed for successful negotiations. These two key dimensions are the "warmth of the relationship" and the "difficulty of getting business."

Traditionally negotiation has an image of confrontation, starting with a low offer and moving slowly and grudgingly. It characterizes many union negotiations. This cold relationship goes hand in hand with difficult business. If you were to chart this style on our Boston matrix, it would sit in the top left quadrant.

On the other hand, you sometime see the reverse situation. A salesman has built up a good working relationship with his customer over time. His company's products have become the standard, and prices have probably edged up in the absence of any competition. This warm

relationship making it easy to get business would therefore sit in the bottom right quadrant. It is fair to say that most negotiations fall into one of these two quadrants.

However, time has shown that there is a better way to negotiate in today's world of business, namely, developing a warm relationship but making business concessions more difficult to come by. This style is very difficult to master but can yield dividends for both sides as it allows for the exploration of different options within the spirit of the relationship.

Although you should aim to spend most of your time in the top right quadrant (quadrant 2), as a top negotiator, you should also be looking to change your behavior to suit the situation.

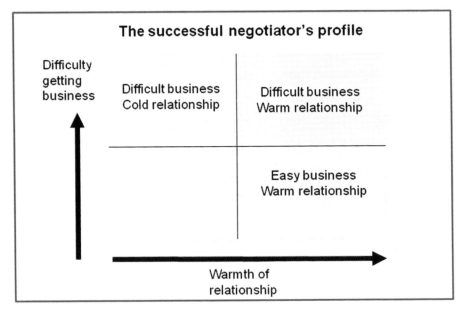

FIGURE 33. THE NEGOTIATOR'S PROFILE

The following guidelines show the key characteristics in both sides of the equation:

Warm relationships	Cold business
<ul><li>Have a positive and creative approach</li><li>Be courteous</li><li>Show an interest by asking good questions</li><li>And listen to the answers</li><li>Admit mistakes or gaps in knowledge</li><li>Look for common ground</li><li>Be adaptable and receptive to new ideas</li></ul>	<ul><li>Preorganization</li><li>Tidy surroundings, clutter free</li><li>Know the subject</li><li>Communicate clearly</li><li>Use the power of silence</li><li>Control of the meeting</li><li>Use your supplier negotiation leverage</li></ul>

FIGURE 34. WARM RELATIONSHIP, COLD BUSINESS

5.3.1 Guiding negotiations

Of all the skills, controlling the negotiation is the most important. And two skills at the heart of this are questioning and listening, with listening being more important that questioning. As the American author James Thurber once said, it is better to know some of the questions than all of the answers. Questions have many different purposes. They are one of the best ways to persuade people; they are a way to gain information, help to plant your ideas with other people, clear up fuzzy thinking, solve problems, take the sting out of criticism, overcome objectives, gain cooperation, and so on.

Seven Types of Questions Useful in Negotiations

Open questions

Most people are familiar with the open question. These are ones that require an answer of more than one word. They are helpful

to get the other party talking. Examples might include, "What are the implications of this?" or "Do you have any suggestions as to how we might improve this next time?"

Closed questions

The opposite of the open question is logically enough the closed question, where you are looking for a single-word answer. These are useful to get absolute clarity about the truth, for example, "Do you think this will be ready on Tuesday?" You often see journalists trying to pin down politicians with a closed question, waiting for a single-word response. For example, "Were you or were you not aware that this was going on?"

Probing questions

Probing questions are the next level up and require a certain amount of skill and sophistication. They invariably use the answer from a previous question to provide an opportunity to ask a secondary question, in effect trying to find out more about a particular situation.

Multiple questions

Multiple questions are quite helpful, where you ask two questions in one. Although this may sound confusing, the effect it has is quite interesting. The person replying hears multiple questions and interprets it often as a request to tell you everything they know about a particular situation. It can be very successful in uncovering hidden information. Oddly, it is very rare that respondents answer the multiple questions clearly and succinctly in order.

Leading questions

Leading questions are famously used by lawyers to get people to admit something they might not otherwise do. An example might be, "Is it not true that you knew you would not be able to meet the delivery times when we placed the order?" Leading questions are often closed questions as they usually require a one-word answer.

Reflective questions

Reflective questions are helpful to calm a meeting down. It might be a way to summarize a situation, for example, "It seems to me that we are going to have to delay this project unless the equipment is delivered earlier." At first sight this sounds like a statement, but it is asking the other party to respond and either agree or explain why this isn't the case.

Hypothetical questions

Finally we have hypothetical questions. This is a very useful tool for the negotiator. Also known as "what if" questions, these are very good for exploring possibilities and suggesting possible trade-offs, for example, "What if we were able to give a two-year commitment? Do you think you would be able to reduce your prices by ten percent?"

TABLE 10. QUESTIONING TYPES

So those are the different types of questions. But questions are not very helpful if they are not joined with good listening skills. The benefits of good listening are significant. It allows the questioner to keep a clear and open mind, understand the key issues more quickly, pick up the real meaning of what is being said, and consequently ask better questions in return. They also improve your status, assuming you don't overuse them, as they provide you with a strong element of control

As a couple of final points, if you are in negotiation, it is really important to have a trusted colleague with you so you can work together. It
can be very difficult to formulate a question accurately at the same time
as you are listening to an answer. Having a partner allows each of you to
think around the situation while the other is asking questions.

5.4 THE NEGOTIATION PROCESS

Now that we have looked at the high-level skills required for good negotiation, let us talk about the different phases of the negotiation. To sim-
plify things it makes sense to think about the negotiation process in six
stages across the three phases (prenegotiation, negotiation, and postne-
gotiation) as in the diagram below:

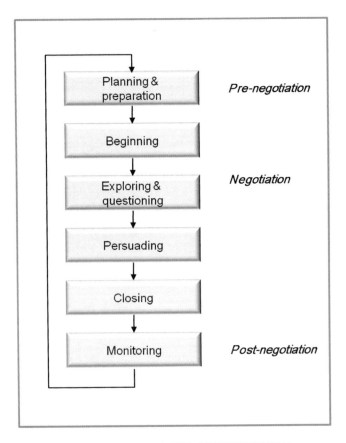

FIGURE 35. THE PROCESS OF NEGOTIATION

5.4.1 Phase 1: Prenegotiation strategy

Very few managers do it, but some planning prior to an IT negotiation makes a huge difference to the outcome. The chart below shows a template that has been used effectively by many IT managers. It helps a negotiation team to understand the goal and priorities of a negotiation. Role plays in our courses highlight in stark contrast the difference in success between those who complete the table and those who don't.

An example of a negotiation strategy

Objective – To reduce our hardware support costs by 10% over the next 3 years, while maintaining support levels for all key applications

Negotiation elements	Priority	Starting position	End position	Supporting arguments
Annual cost	Critical	20% reduced on current pricing	10% on current pricing with 3 year commitment	Market pricing
Service levels	Medium	Maintain for all systems	Maintain for critical systems	Expectation from previous work
Reference	Low (for us)	Do not offer referencability	Offer to act as reference if benefits the deal	Needed to resolve more issues internally

FIGURE 36. NEGOTIATION STRATEGY

The chart above shows how you might build up your negotiation strategy. Start with a statement of your overall negotiation goal. Often this will be a general statement at this time, and you will be able to make it more detailed as you work through the process. In this example we are stating that we want to reduce our hardware support costs with this supplier by 10 percent over the next three years, while maintaining support levels for all key applications.

Draw a table with five columns as shown. Start by listing the individual elements of the negotiation. As we discussed earlier, these may relate to pricing, support, or training as well as other elements. Give each element a priority, and then rank them in order of importance to your business.

Consider what your starting position for this element will be in the negotiation. If you are renegotiating a contract, this will not be the current value unless you feel that the best result you will achieve is to keep the contract at its current level. Think about how far you are prepared to concede on this particular element, and identify what you would consider to be a fair end position.

Finally, prepare your supporting arguments. For example, if you have a hardware support contract and you are looking to get a price reduction, you should be looking for supporting information, such as market pricing (assuming this is falling), similar contracts you have with other suppliers, and so forth. Remember, one of the most powerful tools you will have to achieve your negotiating objectives will be firm and believable evidence to support your position.

Once the table is completed, look at the overall position. Work out what your Best Alternative to a Negotiated Agreement with this party might be—your BATNA. Comparing your BATNA with this negotiation can be quite difficult as not all the variables are comparable. Normally it requires a combination of objective analysis and subjective judgment to determine when you would be better off walking away from the negotiation. Next prepare your overall strategy to meet your end goal. And finally prepare for your first meeting, agreeing on roles and preparing questions ready for negotiation.

5.4.2 Phase 2: Negotiating guidelines

Let us return to the negotiation process. Now that you have prepared your strategy, you need to turn your attention to the negotiation itself.

At the beginning of the process, start the process of conditioning the other party. This is where you effectively communicate your intent. It is often done through the initial correspondence, such as requests for information and invitations to tender. It is important that the intent is consistent throughout the process.

All communications should be managed, not just those in face-to-face meetings. Communications include letters, e-mails, faxes, phone calls, and meetings between all members of your organization and that of the other party. Your negotiation will be undermined, for example, if one of your team tells the supplier that you have no choice but to choose them. But the converse is also true. If you have the opportunity to plant an apparently innocent chance remark that supports your strategy, you might be surprised by the positive impact it has!

Prioritize your arguments with the strongest first. Our role play experiences show very strongly that those who have prepared their strategy properly and understand their priorities in the negotiation come out significantly better off than those that don't.

One of the decisions you face is known as the negotiator's dilemma—the dilemma of knowing where to open. Should you use a shock opening and what might be the consequences? When and how far would you move from your opening position and how long do you hang on?

A useful tip in this situation is to have your opening statement written down. People instinctively believe what is written down more than what is said.

The saying goes that the worst thing you can do to a negotiator is to accept their opening offer. This plays on the fact that when we negotiate, we believe that the process of negotiation is a good thing that will allow us to gain something that we would otherwise not have. Accepting a negotiator's first offer effectively means that the negotiation is finished and the negotiator has no further opportunity to improve their position. But it is a two-way thing. If you accept the first offer, chances are you would also have gained something further through negotiating.

These and some other guidelines for negotiation are summarized in table 11, below.

Guidelines for Negotiation

- Beginning the meeting
  - Prepare an opening statement that outlines what you expect from the negotiation
  - Make a strong impression, and take control
  - Prioritize your arguments (strongest first)
  - Think about where the start the negotiation—your negotiation strategy will help here
  - Don't negotiate grievances—focus on the outcomes you are looking for
  - Create a climate of trust

- Gain information under control
  - Question effectively
  - Listen carefully, always
  - Take time to respond and keep control/calm
  - Don't talk too much
  - Build the relationship

- Keep options open, and look for good outcomes
  - Explore options but stay focused on important issues
  - *Listen* for cues, and *watch* for signals of movement
  - Probe facts, and look for bargaining positions
  - Think creatively about win-win outcomes

- Watch the negotiation concessions
  - Make concessions slowly
  - Always get a concession in return
  - Think clearly when faced with conflict
  - Summarize before moving on
  - Keep a running score

- Deadlock
  - Don't feel pressurized to break a deadlock
  - Don't close them down too early

- Agreeing on a final deal
  - Be wary of "final offers"—keep probing until you are sure
  - Make sure you are satisfied with the balance of concessions before closing (don't worry about fairness; worry about yourself)

- Summarize
  - Play back all of the agreed points in detail
  - Summarize their outcome and next steps
  - Confirm everything in writing

TABLE 11. NEGOTIATION GUIDELINES

The negotiator's most useful word is *if*. Keep using it, for example, "If you were able to reduce your prices by five percent, I believe we would consider acting as a reference site for your new software release," and so on.

Be careful not to overtalk. In our experience overtalking is the biggest mistake that inexperienced negotiators make. It is dangerous for many reasons, not the least that it gives away information that may be of use, but it also gives the other party time to think and takes the pressure off them. There are also certain things that are not advisable to say in the negotiation as they may compromise your bargaining position, such as the following:

- We can't get this anywhere else

- We need it right now

- Our engineers demand your quality

- This is well within our budget!

We talked right at the beginning about the importance of movement in a negotiation. As a negotiator you should try to encourage movement, so listen to what everyone says, and watch for signals, and make openings for the other party to suggest areas of mutual benefit. You may wish to use the principle of the walls of Jericho. The idea here is that if you keep coming around to the same point, even if it is from different angles, eventually the other party will make a concession in that area. This is analogous to Jericho, where the city was circled so many times that eventually the walls collapsed. Examples might include the following:

- Your products are too expensive

- That's more than I paid last year

- The competition gives me better prices

- My budget won't stretch that high

There are still some negotiators who think that offering a concession early in a negotiation will generate a warm and harmonious atmosphere and increase the likelihood of an agreement. This so-called "goodwill conceding" is a myth. It is not true, particularly if you are up against an experienced negotiator. They will merely accept the concession, thank you for it, and wait for the next one. Good negotiators usually make concessions slowly, and if they do make a concession, they make sure they get one back in return.

5.4.3 Phase 2: When it gets too difficult

In a recent IT management course, we ran a complex role play about a company that had bought an expensive management reporting system and had run into problems during the implementation. In essence the idea was that they had bought a solution that was too complex for them to use. The negotiation had several elements:

1. The solution being implemented was too difficult for users to configure their own reports

2. The in-house technical support team did not understand the product well enough to support it

3. The client was refusing to pay its bills

4. The support cost was disproportionately high

In the role play, one team plays the client and the other plays the supplier. Unusually, this group got completely stuck. Both sides were led by competent negotiators, but they kept going around in circles. When we analyzed things retrospectively, we identified some simple but basic principles that need to be followed in this situation:

1. Each side should start by stating its objectives in the negotiation (as per a normal negotiation).

2. Discuss each element in turn—don't expect to agree on each element, but make sure some ideas as to what might be possible are stated by both sides. Each side should use a rational argument to back up their position.

3. When all the elements have been discussed, put forward a straw proposal as to what you would require (based on the individual elemental discussions).

4. Document these, and then discuss the most important differences.

The important outcome here is that you don't need to agree on each element before moving on—just some idea as to what might be possible.

5.4.4 Phase 3: Postnegotiation

To learn from experience, it helps to have a monitoring process in place. Many negotiations will end with a signed contract, and all too often, these are put in a cabinet and forgotten about. Consideration should be given throughout the negotiation to ensuring that the agreement stays living and is flexible enough to meet the changing needs of the customer.

Put in place a review process, taking care to do this before any contract notice period is due so that you don't reduce your negotiating leverage. Finally, have all the necessary facts in front of you prior to this meeting. Resume the conditioning process where you left off. In other words retain consistency in your tough negotiation.

5.5 FINANCE SECRETS FOR IT MANAGERS

Finance is an Achilles' heel for many IT managers, which is nothing if not odd. Most IT professionals have a scientific background and are good with numbers. Maybe it is the jargon that finance people use. Part of it may be the reverse of the problem finance people have with IT. Finance people often want to know the detail and struggle to create an overview model that provides them with what they want. Whatever the reason, what follows is a summary overview of the important financial facts needed by IT managers to do their job.

In the same way that we would not expect finance people to put together technical architectures, IT people shouldn't be running financial spreadsheets and analyses. It is much better to have a financial professional in charge of the process and allow ourselves to oversee the process. This provides a great opportunity to learn more about finance, gets buy-in from the finance department, and ensures that the necessary financial standards are met.

Here are five useful finance techniques for IT managers:

1. Managing budgets: capital investment (capex) and operational expense (opex)

2. Quantifying benefits

3. Calculating return on investment (NPV)

4. Comparing different project business cases (IRR)

5. Sensitivity analysis

5.5.1 Managing IT budgets

One of the key responsibilities of any manager is to manage budgets. As a discipline it is fairly straightforward. Managers are assigned a budget based on what is expected to be a reasonable cost for managing their IT function. Expenditure is logged against the budget and deviations reported. So what could be simpler?

When discussing budgets with the finance department, make sure that budgets can be traced back to the resources needed by a department to fulfill its obligations. Part of this would include an itemized list of support contracts as mentioned earlier, but it may also include a list of staff by subdepartment. So if you have five support staff in ERP application support, the finance department can visualize what this means.

When managing budgets, it is helpful to understand the distinction between capital expenditure (often known as capex) and operational expenditure (known as opex). Operational expenditure is essentially the cost of doing business. Whatever is spent on opex in a year has no value in future months or years. It includes staffing costs and overheads (telephone, stationery, office rental, etc.).

Capital expenditure is investment in the business. Business cases generally require capex as the benefits need to be taken into account

over a longer period for them to be cost effective. Those items bought with capex become assets of the organization. All companies can take advantage of capital allowances that provide tax advantages to encourage investment. However, they are not limitless, so it is possible to exceed the allowance and therefore not get the tax benefit on the full amount of the investment.

The main reason finance treats opex and capex differently is to understand if it the overall business is making money in any month. Investments have a tendency to obscure this, so it makes sense to spread their effect over the period in which the investments are delivering benefits. This is done by depreciating each investment over a period of time, typically three or five years.

By way of example, if you invest in a project in, say, January, and the investment is not spread over a longer period, then obviously your profit and loss figures will look bad. So one of the main points of the capex/opex distinction is to spread the effect of investments and so ensure that profit and loss account represents whether the business continues to be profitable. As a final point, it should be noted that depreciation is to help with management reporting. It is not the basis for company tax returns.

All coherent IT strategies should include both capex and opex budgets. Capex is all about the investments that need to be made to bridge the gap between the current situation and the future state. Although it may only be an estimate, it is important that every project required to deliver success in the future is quantified. Summing up all of these investments will give you the capex budget. Capital budgets therefore are usually a list of expected investments over a period of time (one year for annual capex budgets!). In reality each investment usually needs a specific approval from the capital committee before the project goes ahead. If a capex investment is required to support a reduction in costs, it is important that the two are linked. It would be very dangerous to accept a reduced opex budget without a guarantee of the necessary investment funds to realize it.

One effective technique is to present different scenarios. Each scenario will show how different levels of investment will deliver different levels of operational benefit. How much to spend on IT is a key decision that should be made at the highest levels of an organization. Providing different scenarios will allow the senior management to choose the right balance of investment and performance.

Operational budgets are usually comprised of four main components that require slightly different management:

1. Staff and payroll expenses—make sure these are kept confidential and not itemized in budget calculations!

2. External staff costs—this normally includes contract staff expenses. Keep a careful watch out for expenses here; they can easily spiral out of control. Contractors are typically twice as expensive on an annual basis as full-time staff. If your contractors have been around more than six months, you should be looking to make their functions full-time roles. Contractor expenses can also be high. If possible ask your HR department to help with contractor management

3. Hardware and software support costs—these are usually fixed and payable either annually, quarterly, or monthly. It is important to have all these support costs itemized on a contract-by-contract basis. This is very helpful in budget discussions. Finance departments often ask for cost savings. Since many of your contract support costs are fixed and may not be negotiable, the discretionary part of your budget may actually be quite small. Similarly, cost of living adjustments may be due on some of your support contracts. Having an accurate list of what the budget is being spent on will serve you well in such discussions.

4. Other costs—these may include an apportioned amount of overheads, including office space, data centers, etc. It is often worth reviewing these costs as allocations from other departments have a habit of ending up here. These may be unauthorized hardware or software purchases.

5.5.2 Business benefits

There is almost a subculture about calculating business benefits so that organizations can verify that projects are delivering on their promises. The fact is that calculating benefits is very simple in theory and difficult in practice. The aim is to find the net contribution that a particular benefit will deliver for an organization. This net contribution then becomes the input figure for a return on investment calculation. The statement "net contribution" is important. The important thing to measure here then is the difference between the benefits of keeping the existing systems versus the benefit of a new project (typically the implementation of a new system). It is perfectly possible that doing nothing is actually losing the company money. It might be that the implementation of a new system is required just to keep the company where it is now, to, for example, maintain a particular market share. Even though the revenue of the company is staying constant, the net benefit is positive.

The second point about business benefits is that not all business benefits are the same. Accountants consider four types of benefit in the following descending order of importance:

1. The best kind of benefit from the accountant's perspective is the cost saving objective. Typical examples of cost saving objectives might be reducing contract staff levels, reducing (ongoing) purchase costs, or reducing support costs.

2. The second benefits are efficiency objectives, such as reducing process steps or consolidating systems, making the company efficient, and in turn saving internal or external labor costs. This benefit is not as high as the raw cost saving benefit as there is usually work to realize the staff reduction saving, and in some cases, this may not be possible.

3. The third type is the business growth objectives (predictive). These might include growing new markets or improving revenue levels. These are considered relatively risky by finance people as there are many reasons why they might not be realized. They are also quite difficult to measure. For example, if you put in a new prospect management system and sales levels grow by 10 percent over the next year, was this due to the new system or an overall growth in the market? It is difficult to tell.

4. The final type of benefit is the intangible benefit. Accountants really don't like these at all, and where possible, equivalent tangible benefits should be identified. Examples of an intangible benefit might be customer satisfaction or employee satisfaction. However, if possible you should look at how improving customer satisfaction or employee satisfaction might improve the business. If you take the case of employee satisfaction, perhaps there is a correlation between employee satisfaction and employee retention and you can calculate the value of employee retention by working out how much recruitment costs. If you pin some financial value to this benefit, you need to have some way to identify which that this benefit was specifically due to your project success. However, in some cases you just need to recognize that you won't be able to quantify the reasons for doing a particular project, but you just know it is the "right" thing to do.

5.5.3 Calculating a business case

An investment business case is calculated by establishing the difference between "doing something," in other words making the investment, and "doing nothing." The most straightforward way of expressing this is via the cash flow model. Each company has its own standards, and you should always work with your finance department when preparing business cases, but they follow the same broad principles.

PETER'S STORY

The capital committee in our company had something of a reputation for being a tough act. Each week managers would present their business cases for investment approval. We would each be given a fifteen-minute slot. Prior to our presentation, we had to complete a detailed capital approval request showing what the investment was required for, how much it would cost, the payback period, project time scales, risks, and so on. Probably the same as every other major corporate organization.

The first time I went in, it was very daunting, and it didn't go well. I went through the capital approval form to a sea of intense and yet at the same time bored faces. I stumbled over some of the details, and had my project rejected. It was only after I discussed the paper with the finance department that I realized my mistake. We had underplayed some of the benefits, and although the business case looked pretty impressive to me, it clearly wasn't as impressive as some of the others in front of the committee. What I had failed to notice was that there was only so much investment capital money available. A business case would not be approved purely based on a positive return on investment. There was the opportunity cost—in other words, was there another project with a better return on investment that would make better use of limited resources?

There were other factors that came into the equation. What I learned, though, was that mathematics wasn't enough to secure funding for an investment project. There was a lot I needed to know about the financial side of the business and the political priorities of the senior managers.

Let us take the following example (assume all costs are in thousands of pounds). We have decided to invest in a new IT system that will cost $60,000 up front for the initial investment, with annual support costs expected to be $5,000 thereafter. This is represented in the top line of the table shown here.

	Year 0	Year 1	Year 2	Year 3	Year 4
Costs	60	5	5	5	5
Benefits	0	20	25	30	25
Net benefit for the year	-60	15	20	25	20
Cash flow	-60	-45	-25	0	20

TABLE 12. BUSINESS CASE CALCULATIONS

The year numbering is important. The $60,000 is shown as year 0. This is accountant's shorthand for today. Year 1 then includes the costs in the next twelve months and so on. We have looked at the benefits that this project will deliver us. We will talk later to the different types of benefit, but let us for now assume that they are as shown here. Clearly we won't see any benefit on the day we sign the contract, so the year 0 benefit is zero. But we might expect some benefit in year 1. We have assumed this is $20,000 rising to $25,000 in year 2, $30,000 in year 3, and starting to tail off to $25,000 in year 4 as the system starts to reach the end of its life.

We can now calculate the net benefit for each period, subtracting the cost from the benefit. This means a net loss on the day we sign the contract. Remember that this is a cash flow calculation, and this is what you would expect. Your bank will be debited with the $60,000. Soon the project will start delivering more benefit than it costs, so in year 1, we see a net benefit of $15,000. Now let us look at the overall cash flow position. We were $60,000 down on the first day but recouped $15,000 at the end of the first year, so we are only down by $45,000 at the end of year 1. Another $20,000 comes in year 2, and therefore our position improves further. We have still spent more than we have gained, but we are only down $25,000 on the project to date by the end of year 2. In year 3 we break even, having recouped all of the $60,000 investment with the benefits from the first three years. And happily we start to make an overall gain by the end of year 4.

The previous table is the simplest representation of a cost/benefit analysis. The problem is that it does not account for the "time value of money." The principle of the time value of money states that money received in the future is not as useful as money received today—by an amount equal to the interest rate, also known as the "discount rate." To make the calculation reflect reality, you have to convert the future benefits to today's values. This is done by using a discount factor, which adjusts the amount that they would have gained just from the interest growth. In UK currency for example, $1 today will be worth $\$(1 + i)^n$ (where i is the annual interest rate and n is the number of years) in any future year. To normalize it to the correct value, future benefits therefore have to be discounted by a discount factor $1 / (1 + i)^n$. The interest rate i is more accurately called the discount rate.

In the example below, we have used a discount rate of 6% or $i = 0.06$. We can then calculate the discount factors for the different years. For today, when $n = 0$, this makes the discount factor 1, which is what you would expect. For the end of year 1, the discount factor $= 1 / (1 + 0.06) = 0.94$ (to two decimal points). For the end of year 2, this is $0.94^2 = 0.89$.

	Year 0	Year 1	Year 2	Year 3	Year 4
Costs	60	5	5	5	5
Benefits	0	20	25	30	25
Net benefit (for the year)	-60	15	20	25	20
Discount factor	1	0.94	0.89	0.84	0.79
Discounted benefit	-60	14.1	17.8	21.0	15.8
Net present value	-60	-45.9	-28.1	-7.1	+8.7

TABLE 13. DISCOUNTED CASH FLOW

To summarize, we repeat our example from earlier with an interest rate or discount rate of 6 percent. This corresponds to a discount factor of $1 / (1 + 0.06)^n$ after year n. The discount factors for the different years

are given in row 5 of the table. We now need to reduce the predicted benefits by the corresponding discount factors. This gives us row 6. The benefit of $15,000 from year 1, for example, is multiplied by 0.94 to give a discounted benefit of approximately $14,100. The other benefits are discounted as shown using the different factors. Finally, we accumulate the benefits over the different years to give a discounted cash flow, to provide what is commonly known as the net present value (NPV). NPV is a popular way for finance people to measure the overall benefit of a project over a particular time period.

So we have just done what is called a discounted cash flow forecast. Different companies do these slightly differently, so it is worth you speaking to your finance people should you need to prepare an investment business case. As mentioned earlier it is much more valuable for finance to do the business case as they will ensure it follows the company accounting and financial standards and will stand behind the figures at your capital committee or equivalent approval body.

As you can see from the previous calculation, incorporating the discount factor in the model makes a significant difference to the business case. Specifically, in the previous example, the net present value over four years has reduced from $20,000 with a discount rate of zero to $6,700 with a discount rate of 6 percent. Remember, it is important to provide the time units for NPV. For example, saying a business case has an NPV of $6,700 is only meaningful if you let people know that it is for a four-year period.

5.5.4 Comparing different business cases

Although accountants prefer to talk about NPV, there is another measure that can be helpful, called internal rate of return or IRR. IRR is useful because it allows you to compare projects of different sizes. Naturally you would expect a larger project to have a higher NPV than a smaller one. But it is not always easy to see whether the bigger project is providing the better return on investment.

IRR overcomes some of these problems as it uses a percentage comparison rather than the total benefit. It is basically defined as the maximum discount rate that the project could withstand before the NPV falls to zero. It can be thought of as similar (but not quite the same) as the equivalent investment to the bank interest rate. So for example a project with an IRR of 10 percent is similar to getting a 10 percent rate of return from the bank.

IRR can also be understood as follows: If all the money for the project development were borrowed and the project broke even, then the interest paid on that borrowed money would be the IRR. To calculate it, keep increasing the interest rate gradually up to the point when the NPV becomes zero. The interest or discount rate at which this occurs is known as the internal rate of return. Calculating the IRR is usually an iterative process. Fortunately, in Excel, there is a function called IRR. Its syntax is to enter " = (range of net undiscounted cash flows).

One final point on IRR: IRRs on projects normally need to be much higher than investment returns. This is because the treasury department of your organization will have a much higher cost of capital than just the interest rate return. In addition, a significant contingency needs to be added to take account of the risk of the project. Finally, different projects will be competing for available investment money, and hence the threshold (sometimes called the hurdle rate) is normally nearer 20 percent. Again your finance department should be able to provide some guidelines on the expected benefits from business cases.

5.5.5 Sensitivity analysis

It must be remembered that the figures used for some costs and most benefits are estimated. Without realizing it, it is possible to put forward a business case that is highly dependent on one assumption. If this assumption is a bit uncertain, you should seriously consider not doing it. Finding out if there are key benefits that have no margin for error, as it were, is an important part of the business approval process.

One way to assess the robustness of the business case is by using a technique called GAP analysis. GAP (good, average, poor), sometimes known as Best, Most likely, Worst case. It is calculated taking into account estimating inaccuracies, allowances for known risks, and an overall tolerance.

The business case GAP will narrow as the project progresses and more certainty is established. It is helpful to identify the sensitive areas of the business case that are more risky and need closer management and control. Leading organizations review business cases after implementation. If possible you should have a review process for your projects, ideally as part of a project portfolio management system.

As a final point, if you are part of a business case or capital approval committee, you will be used to reviewing many different business cases. All business cases that are put forward will have compelling reasons for going ahead. However, you will soon realize that your role on the committee is not to look at the numbers and approve those with the highest NPV or IRR. Your role is to test the assumptions in the business case and make relative judgments as to which are the best projects to allocate precious resources to. The GAP analysis described here is one of the best ways to see how robust the projects being put before you for approval are.

6. In Conclusion

6.1 TAKE TIME TO REFLECT

THIS BOOK CAN ONLY PROVIDE A SUMMARY OF IT MANAGEMENT AND OFFERS PROVEN GUIDELINES THAT WE HAVE FOUND WORK well. Depending on your current role, company, or situation, some ideas will be more relevant than others. Look to develop your own thinking in this area, adapted to your own style and your organization.

6.2 NEXT STEPS

Based on this review, identify some areas to improve your performance. Think about your own career development and that of your team. Consider what would have the most significant impact on performance and be easy to implement. Then make a simple to-do list with timings for completion.

6.3 AND FINALLY

If you found this book valuable or would like some advice on any of the topics, please feel free to e-mail me at david.mckean@itleaders.co.uk.

Good luck!
David McKean

7. Bibliography

FOLLOWING ARE SOME RECOMMENDED BOOKS AND PAPERS THAT HAVE BEEN SOURCES OF KNOWLEDGE AND INSPIRATION.

IT STRATEGIST

David McKean. *Strategy, Fast Track to Success.* Financial Times/ Prentice Hall, 2012
The book outlines a ten-step business strategy process and some of the leading ideas and techiques from the world of business strategy.

Michael E *Porter, "What Is Strategy?" Harvard Business Review* (product no. 4134)
A classic paper of the key principles of developing corporate strategy

Richard Tanner Pascale and Anthony Athos. *The Art of Japanese Management.* Simon & Schuster. 1981
Explanation of the 7-S model, which is used by McKinsey in their strategy consulting, and looks at how Japanese companies assign considerable importance to both hard and soft aspects of management

Robert Kaplan and David Norton. *The Balanced Scorecard.* Harvard Business Review Press, 1996
A best-selling business book on how to make sure you measure the right metrics in your business to maintain competitive advantage.

Robert Kaplan and David Norton. *The Strategy-Focused Organization*. Harvard Business Review Press, 2000
The second book by Kaplan and Norton after their success with The Balanced Scorecard, which explains how to use the balanced scorecard method as a foundation for developing effective business (and IT) strategy

Tregoe and Zimmerman. *Top Level Strategy*. Pocket Books, 1983
A great book looking at the strategic driving force in organizations and creating competitive advantage

W.C. Kim and R. Mauborgne. "Charting Your Company's Future." *Harvard Business Review*, June 2002
Kim and Mauborgne pioneered the technique of a strategic canvass for mapping out strategy.

W.C. Kim and R. Mauborgne. *Blue Ocean Strategy*. Harvard Business Review Press, 2004
Blue Ocean Strategy explains the importance of creating competitive advantage and barriers to entry and how to look at markets in different ways to identify new business opportunities.

Ethan Rasiel. *The McKinsey Way*. New York: McGraw-Hill, 1999.
The McKinsey Way explains the approach McKinsey consultants take to solving business problems, including details on the importance of the principle MECE (Mutually exclusive, collectively exhaustive)

CHANGE LEADER

Iain Begg. "Don't lose your RAG." *IMB Consulting*
Iain Begg is a leading consultant on project management. The full paper is available, free to download at www.imb-consulting.co.uk

Charles Pellerin. *How NASA Builds Teams*. Wiley, 2009
Charles Pellerin explains how NASA builds teams and how different leadership personalities shape teams. It also examines the importance of

social context in running successful teams, building trust and enabling team members to discuss problems openly.

Project Management Institute. *A Guide to the Project Management Book of Knowledge (PMBOK)*. PMI, 2013.
This book is an industry standard reference and contains everything you might wish to know about the structured management of projects.

Onckon and Wass. "Who's got the monkey." *Harvard Business Review*, reprint 99609
An important paper on avoiding getting involved in problems that aren't yours!

Iain Begg. "Avoiding Project Sponsorship becoming a spectator sport." *IMB Consulting*
Iain Begg is a leading consultant on project management. The full paper available, free to download at www.imb-consulting.co.uk

Keith Baxter. *Risk Management, Fast Track to Success*. Financial Times/ Prentice Hall, 2012
A fuller description of assumption-based risk management, QBC, and Monte Carlo analysis is given in *Risk Management Fast Track to Success*, by Keith Baxter.

John Kotter. *Leading Change.* Harvard Business Press, 2012
An excellent book explaining eight key guidelines for successful business change.

John Kotter. *The Heart of Change*. Harvard Business Press, 2012.
In this second book by John Kotter, some great examples are narrated, showing the eight key principles of change management in practice.

PERFORMANCE PIONEER

Jeffrey Liker. *The Toyota Way*. McGraw-Hill, 2003

The Toyota Way discusses the LEAN process as it was development by the Toyota Company. The Toyota Way looks at the key principles for running an efficient manufacturing operation. LEAN doesn't claim to eliminate production problems, merely to continually improve quality and reduce the likelihood of problems.

Greg Brue. *Six Sigma for Managers*. McGraw-Hill, 2005
A good introduction to the subject, this book is highly readable and includes twenty-four lessons to understand and apply Six Sigma principles in any organization

CRISIS COMMANDER

Maiwald and Sieglein. *Security Planning and Disaster Recovery*. Osborne/McGraw-Hill, 2002
This is a manual on managing security and gives a structured process, including checklists at the end of each chapter. There aren't many laughs in it, but it is comprehensive.

Nassim Nicholas Taleb. *The Black Swan, The Impact of the Highly Improbable*. Penguin, 2008
Black Swans, events that come as a complete surprise but were in fact perfectly predictable, have come into prominence recently, as people have been looking at the reasons behind the financial crisis and the risk management processes. A good account of the subject.

Charles Kepner and Benjamin Tregoe. *The New Rational Manager*. Kepner-Tregoe, 1997
This was a ground-breaking book on management effectiveness, and follows the authors' extensive research, identifying the key techniques of the top US companies with a view to translating them to other businesses. The book is a good read and is as relevant today as when it was written.

COMMERCIAL EXPERT

Gavin Kennedy. *Everything's Negotiable*. Cornerstone Digital, 2010
A highly readable book on negotiation. Each chapter has an interesting set of negotiation questions to test your knowledge.

Fisher and Ury with Bruce Patton. *Getting to Yes: Negotiating an Agreement Without Giving In*. Cornerstone Digital, 2012
A classic book on negotiation techniques.

Kate Vitasek. *The Vested Outsourcing Manual*. Palgrave Macmillan, 2011
A guide for creating successful business and outsourcing agreements.

Paul Klinger and Rachael Burnett. *Drafting and Negotiating IT Contracts*. Bloomsbury Professional, 2013.
A readable book with extensive practical guidelines.

Ken Langdon and Alan Bonham. *Smart Finance*. Capstone, 2004
An excellent general introduction to finance

31225121R00121

Made in the USA
Charleston, SC
08 July 2014